D1142251

TEDBooks

Rescue

Refugees and the Political Crisis of Our Time

DAVID MILIBAND

TED Books
Simon & Schuster

London New York Toronto Sydney New Delhi

First published in Great Britain by Simon & Schuster UK Ltd, 2017
A CBS COMPANY

First TED Books hardback edition October 2017

TED, the TED logo and TED Books are trademarks of TED Conference, LLC.
TED BOOKS and colophon are registered trademarks of TED Conferences, LLC.

For more information on licensing the TED talk that accompanies this book,
or other content partnerships with TED, please contact TEDBooks@TED.com.

10 9 8 7 6 5 4 3 2 1

Simon & Schuster UK Ltd
1st Floor
222 Gray's Inn Road
London WC1X 8HB

www.simonandschuster.co.uk
www.simonandschuster.com.au
www.simonandschuster.co.in

Simon & Schuster Australia, Sydney
Simon & Schuster India, New Delhi

The author and publishers have made all reasonable effort to contact
copyright-holders for permission, and apologise for any omissions or errors
in the form of credits given. Corrections may be made to future printings.

A CIP catalogue record for this book
is available from the British Library

Hardback ISBN: 978-1-4711-7048-5
eBook ISBN: 978-1-4711-7049-2

Interior design by: MGMT.design
Jacket design by: MGMT.design

Printed and bound by CPI Group (UK) Ltd, Croydon, CR0 4YY

Simon & Schuster UK are committed to sourcing paper that is made
from wood grown in sustainable forests and support the Forest Stewardship
Council, the leading international forest certification organisation. Our
books displaying the FSC logo are printed on FSC certified paper.

For Louise, my loving refuge,
and for Isaac and Jacob, my wonderful escape

CONTENTS

INTRODUCTION   1

CHAPTER 1
The Crisis   24

CHAPTER 2
Why We Should Care   43

CHAPTER 3
The Renewal of Rescue   67

CHAPTER 4
Refugees Welcome   91

CHAPTER 5
Conclusion   109

ACKNOWLEDGMENTS   126
NOTES   129

Rescue

The first refugees I ever met were my parents.

My father came to the United Kingdom as a refugee from Belgium in 1940. The day the Germans invaded, he and his father fled their home in Brussels. Walking and hitching rides, they made it to the port of Ostende and got on the last boat out of Belgium. In Britain, my father flourished. He learned English, graduated from secondary school in west London, qualified for the London School of Economics, and after a year of university joined the Royal Navy. He worked at sea on the "cans"—headphones used to listen to intercepts of German messaging. As a boy, I would feel great pride when he told me stories of the D-Day landings: he said that wherever you looked in the dawn light on June 6, 1944, there were boats of all shapes and sizes, so many that you could hardly see the sea.

My mother has her own refugee story, one that starts in Poland. She survived the war with her mother and sister, hiding first in a convent and then with an incredibly brave Warsaw family who welcomed her in. In 1946, her mother sent her to the United Kingdom to start a new life. Her father, David, was killed in the war. No one really talked about him when I was young. However, recently a German history group wrote to say that there was new confirmation that David

Kozak had been sent from Auschwitz to Hailfingen concentration camp near Stuttgart toward the end of 1944. He died there in 1945.

My parents did what is most important to so many refugees: they gave their children the security they themselves had never had. My dad was nine when Adolf Hitler came to power in Germany; sixteen when the Nazis invaded his homeland and he fled to Great Britain; twenty-one when the war ended. The rise of fascism was the shadow over his childhood. My mother was five when she first had to go into hiding, seven when she was saved by the Warsaw family who pretended she was a relative, twelve when her mother put her on a boat to Britain with a group of Polish Jewish orphans. They were promised, and given, a new start in life by a prominent British rabbi, Solomon Schonfeld.

My parents ensured that I had none of these concerns. We were a middle-class, albeit foreign, British family. We were conscious of being Jewish but were not conspicuously so: no synagogue, no bar mitzvah. When I was nine in 1974, the big question for me was how Holland had lost the football (soccer) World Cup final to West Germany (which won 2 to 1). In a middle-class family, I was protected from the harsh winds of the Margaret Thatcher revolution in the United Kingdom: when I went to university in the mid-1980s, we were protesting against the introduction of university tuition fees, not paying them.

This personal backstory deeply affects how I see the refugee crisis. It makes real the idea that "it could be me." For me, my family's experiences have turned refugees from a faceless category into blood and spirit. It demonstrates how our lives depend on the decisions of strangers.

In February 2017, I went to Khazer camp in Iraq, around 30 kilometers (18 miles) from Mosul, to meet people fleeing from the so-called Islamic State (I use the Arabic term Daesh in this book) as Iraqi forces retook the city. I met Nabil and Amira. They were sitting on a mattress in a tent—their new home in the camp.[1] They had nothing beyond the clothes they wore and carried, plus their memories and their fears. They told me about their daughter, still trapped in Mosul. She was married to a man who used to work for the Iraqi military. For that reason he had been forced to live underground in Mosul for more than two years for fear of being found by Daesh and executed. I couldn't hear their story without thinking of the perils faced by my own mother.

In another tent I met the Ibrahim family—a husband and wife with three wide-eyed daughters. "We ran a hundred meters to the Iraqi troops, but it felt like it took a year to get there," they told me. My thoughts turned to my dad and granddad making the 71-mile trip from Brussels to Ostende to board a boat to Britain.

Today's refugees are a different religion from my family. Their circumstances are different, and world politics are different. But they, too, are fleeing war and persecution. They, too, have lost all the security they ever had, left everything familiar—home, culture, family, work—and risked their lives to reach safety. And the questions raised by their desperate flight are the same: How to eat, sleep, survive? How to start anew? Whom to trust?

One question stands above all others. It is a question to us who are not refugees: What are the duties of the rest of the world toward the innocent victims of war? What are our duties to strangers? That is what this book is about: the lives of 65 million people displaced by conflict and persecution in places such as Syria, Afghanistan, and Democratic Republic of Congo (DRC), and what our responsibilities are to them.

The Crisis

Crisis is an overused word, but the massive forced displacement we see today, the sheer number of people driven from their homes by war or oppression, deserves that description. This is a global crisis.

We are witnessing the largest flow of people fleeing for their lives since the Second World War. In total, they account for 1 in every 113 people on the planet.[2] If they came together as a single country, it would be the world's twenty-first largest[3] (about the size of the United Kingdom).

In the pages that follow, you will meet South Sudanese fleeing violence in the world's newest nation to find safety across the border in Uganda, Syrians seeking respite in Jordan from the bombings by their own president, Nigerians seeking protection from the terror group Boko Haram. The scale of forced displacement is both a symptom and a cause of a world in disarray.[4] A symptom because it is a product of failed governance within nations and failed promises in the so-called international community; a cause because of the political instability that can come in its wake.

These refugees and displaced people are fleeing wars *within* states. Since the collapse of the Soviet Union and the end of the Cold War at the end of the 1980s, the number of civil wars has risen tenfold from the average between 1816 and 1989.[5]

If the crisis were a blip, it might be considered immoral to hunker down and hope that the storm passes, but it would not have a global significance beyond that. However, civil wars have become increasingly long, and they are devastating for civilians caught in the cross fire. I believe we are seeing a trend, not a blip, driven by long-term factors that have not yet played out.

There are a growing number of countries where political institutions are unable to contain the needs and aspirations of different ethnic, political, or religious groups within peaceful boundaries. The result is conflict that combines with poverty and weak governance to create huge movements of people. Meanwhile, international institutions of political coordination and consensus building, led by the United Nations, are weaker, relative to the problems that need to be tackled, than at any time since they were created after the Second

World War. The political scientist Ian Bremmer has called it a "leaderless world."[6] Another way of looking at it is that with the dispersion of economic power there are too many leaders today and no one in charge.

This crisis is large scale and not going away. It has deep roots and complex consequences that challenge the way aid has been provided to refugees in the past. If the refugee crisis is not managed better, it will cause more instability as well as more suffering.

Rescue Us

Refugees and displaced people have lost everything. But the refugee crisis is not just about "them"; it is also about "us"— what we, living in far greater comfort, stand for and how we see our place in the world. It is a test of our character, not just our policies. Pass the test, and we rescue ourselves and our values as well as refugees and their lives.

I lead an organization dedicated to helping refugees and displaced people called the International Rescue Committee (IRC). We have 27,000 staff and volunteers working in thirty war-affected countries. More than 90 percent of the IRC's staff are from countries that are directly affected by conflict and disaster. We don't have to persuade them to go toward danger and tumult; they are working to make a difference in their own communities. They deliver humanitarian aid: health care, water and sanitation, education, employment, protection from harm. In twenty-six US cities we also help resettled refugees start new lives: meeting them at the airport, helping their kids into school, finding them work. The work of my colleagues is a daily lesson in ingenuity and commitment across the arc of crisis, from harm to home.

The work of the IRC stands on the shoulders of some of the giants of the Western world in the twentieth century. In his native Germany, Albert Einstein was accused of treason by the Nazis. His theory of relativity was branded "Jewish physics." His books were burned in a purging of "un-German" spirit. After fleeing to the United States in October 1933, he said, "I am almost ashamed to be living in such peace while the rest struggle and suffer." One thing he did was help found the IRC.

●　　●　　●

After the Second World War, refugee law and refugee protection were promoted by Western leaders who said "never again" to statelessness, estrangement, and hopelessness for the civilian victims of war. The work of rescue depends in large part on the mind-set of citizens and leaders in the countries that for eighty years have set global rules, upheld global norms, and funded global humanitarian efforts. Yet today the mood is both bitter and contested. Syrian refugees are demonized in a US presidential campaign. Foreign aid is called unaffordable and worse. Refugees are featured as a reason for the United Kingdom to leave the European Union and are walled out of Europe.

At issue is whether the sixty-five years that have passed between the 1951 UN Refugee Convention and the present day are an aberration or whether the Enlightenment ideal of treating strangers like brothers (and sisters) can be maintained. I believe that it both can and must: by maintaining the integrity of the refugee system; by humanizing the plight of refugee populations; by explaining the strategic need to support states such as Jordan, Pakistan, and Ethiopia that are dealing with large numbers of refugees; and by welcoming refugees to our own countries and embracing them in our places of work, in our centers of worship, and around our dinner tables.

It is clear to me that refugees are victims of terror, not terrorists themselves; that their situation is not so dire that it cannot be improved; and that if we do not address their situation, it will mean not only misery for them but shame and trouble for us.

Our challenge is not just to rescue those in need; it is to rescue and renew the values of international engagement and mutual respect that have been essential to the things that Western countries have done right over the last eighty years—practices which became the global standard in international conventions and which ultimately define who we are, how strong our societies are, and what leverage we exert around the world.

This case has not been made with sufficient vigor or clarity, and the danger is that it is being lost by default. That came home to me in Silicon Valley in February 2017 when I addressed a booming and brilliant software company whose staff were outraged by the crackdown on immigrants and refugees ordered by President Donald Trump on January 27, 2017. At that time, I told the group that the proposed US ban on visitors from seven (subsequently reduced to six) Muslim countries and the 120-day ban on all refugees pending a review of vetting arrangements were not just the result of an election; they were the product of forty years of confusion, and to some extent complacency, about who refugees are, why they are displaced, and how they are related to but separate from the global trend toward increased migration.

There is no excuse anymore. The Syrian civil war is widely recognized as one of the great human as well as political tragedies of the modern world. The civil wars in Afghanistan, DRC, and Somalia have been burning for a generation. New conflicts in South Sudan, Niger, and Nigeria have added to the toll. In each case there has been widespread killing but also a massive exodus of people. And the power of modern social media means that we can see what is happening on our smartphones in real time.

•   •   •

I want to counter the view that sees this great global problem as insoluble. I want more people to understand and support refugees and displaced people. And although I have gone from being a politician covering a wide canvas to a leader of a humanitarian NGO, I want to make the link between the cause of forcibly displaced people and the strength of a liberal, democratic international order, which has given me my life chances and which I believe is the best hope for humankind.

The choices are urgent. For the refugees and displaced people, the needs are pressing. And for Western democracies, our moral and strategic character is on the line. Fail the refugees, and we fail ourselves.

Politics

In 2013, I made a big life change: I left UK politics and went into the NGO sector, joining the IRC in New York. I saw it as a way to bring my values, my family history, and my professional skills together. I want to return briefly to my time in politics and government because of how the lessons learned there have come to bear on my current work and understanding of the refugee crisis.

My heart always beat on the left of politics—to make the privileges and choices of the few the experience of the many. I first began to understand inequality of opportunity at school, when some classmates left at age fifteen without taking any exams. Social justice would not be an add-on for me; it was fundamental. My brain told me that changing the world meant developing ideas that people would support.

I became involved near the top of British politics in 1994, when the leader of the opposition, Tony Blair, asked me to head up the policy operation for his office. My party, Labour, had lost four elections in a row, and my job was to weed out the policies that wouldn't work and would cost us votes, and find the policies that were impactful and popular. I was twenty-nine at the time, and I had the opportunity to watch, and make a contribution to, the life of my party and country.

The next seven years, with two landslide majorities in 1997 and 2001, were the most successful period of peacetime politics the Labour Party has ever enjoyed. One of the least successful social democratic parties in Europe in the twentieth century suddenly became one of the most successful—in electoral terms and in some ways in policy terms.

There is a lot of revisionist history about that period in government. Often it alleges that there was no deviation from the politics of Margaret Thatcher—a smaller state, deregulation, and the like. But the facts do not bear that out. On public spending, labor market regulation (minimum wage, employee protection), and tackling poverty, never mind social reform in the area of women's rights and gay rights, and on European policy, overseas aid, and constitutional reform, the governments of that period set a different trajectory for the country. I know Iraq became a disastrous icon of our period in government, and I speak about it in the pages to come, but it is far from the whole story. Though it is reasonable to argue that we should have done more, and in the case of financial regulation done things differently, it is not true that we made no difference. I balk when our time in office is called "Tory lite." I believe we ultimately ran into the sand because of a failure to adapt, refresh, and build on what had been achieved—not because the voters couldn't tell the difference between us and the Conservatives.

There were many lessons, some of which we learned the hard way. For example, it is easy for a government, consumed by the business of making and delivering policy, to allow the story of its purpose and values to be lost. That happened in the successful emergency response to the economic crisis in 2008–9. People thought we had "saved the bankers" when in fact we had protected the livelihoods of the population. There were lessons, too, about the need to follow policy all the way through to the front line to make real change, the madness created by trying to manage the media, and the need to reform and invigorate party structures out of government at the same time as you are grappling with reform of government itself.

But the most important lesson was about the difference between knowing your own mind and constructing your own version of reality. It explains to me the difference between politicians who succeed and those who fail. If you can't stand outside your own mind-set and recognize its flaws as well as strengths, you end up sunk, because you can no longer see the point of view of the voter. As a staffer, your job is to help keep your boss on the right side of the line, opening the shutters, keeping the ideas flowing, analyzing and bomb-proofing your own arguments. And of course the greater the political success, the greater the importance and difficulty of challenging the groupthink that crowds in on successful political projects.

Before the 2001 election, Tony persuaded me that I should go into Parliament and helped me become an elected member of Parliament for South Shields in the northeast of England. This kind of move, sometimes referred to as "parachuting," is often criticized, because it brings outsiders into traditional Labour communities. But the critique is valid only if the new MP thinks he or she knows everything and behaves like a representative of the Empire to the colonies. I found that people in South Shields cared about whether I could deliver for them, not where I came from.

The ex-mining and ex-shipbuilding community was new to me. I remember going up onstage on a Saturday night, in between two sets from a local band, at the Cleadon Social Club—formerly a workingmen's club but now admitting women. There must have been 150 people in the room, in the main middle-aged and above, gathered in groups of four or five around small tables. There was some domino playing, some bingo, some cards, and some drinking. It was smoky (this was before the smoking ban). I went round introducing myself as the new Labour candidate. Then I had to go onstage. I can still feel a bit of the cringe as I stood there in my suit and glasses and tried to explain who I was, what I hoped to do for South Shields, and why I wanted their votes. But people didn't care about my suit or my glasses. Their position was: "Show us what you can do."

South Shields became a whole new part of my life. I came to treasure my relationships there. The people reminded me of some things I had learned when we lived in a small town outside Leeds in the 1970s: that community really means something, that life for people at the sharp end involves the hardest choices, that respect is the foundation of representation, that who you are as a person is critical to what you do as a politician. I still have a special feeling when I go back.

In 2002, I was made minister for schools, starting a period of eight years when I sat on the front bench of British government. After a year in charge of local government after the 2005 election, I became environment secretary in 2006 and then started three years as foreign secretary in Gordon Brown's government in 2007. I always say that government has more power than an NGO but more obstacles in its way. Those obstacles, some of them valuable checks on executive power, are worth overcoming because the potential to make a positive difference in people's lives is so great. The fuel for my politics was the children's education we were supporting, the cities we were empowering, and the international leadership, first environmental and then on a broader canvas, we were offering. My approach was to rally people affected by the issues around big goals: rebuilding every secondary school in the country, giving more power to "city regions," binding future governments to reduce greenhouse gas emissions through climate change legislation, peacemaking in the Balkans.

Leading a government department is a challenge like no other, because of the multiple bottom lines on which you are judged: developing policies to make the country better, then seeing whether they do make it better; competing with the opposition to win your case; holding your own with the media, which can make you or break you; cooperating with colleagues who can also see you as a rival; bringing pride to your departmental civil servants without falling victim to Stockholm syndrome. I found the sense of possibility invigorating. I developed my views in government, honed my view of leadership, and reaffirmed my values.

When I was foreign secretary, we continued to live at home (not at the official residence, 1 Carlton Gardens, next to the headquarters of General Charles de Gaulle during the Second World War). We kept our network of friends. But there is no point pretending. It is weird to have twenty-four-hour guards with machine guns standing outside your house and a security team walking on the other side of the road as you take your kids to school. It is unusual to have your own police code word—mine was "MetPol 704"—that the protection team would whisper into their sleeves as we drove home in the evening. And it is an extraordinary privilege to be able to invite your friends and their children to an Easter egg hunt in the 2,000-acre grounds of a seventeenth-century house outside London (Chevening) that the foreign secretary is allowed to use at weekends. In Britain there were no government planes, but we did have houses.

The Labour government lost the 2010 general election for reasons that deserve another book. I also lost a second election in 2010, for the Labour Party leadership, to my brother, Ed. It is tough to think back to that period, because the campaign and its results were so negative, both short term and long term, both personally and politically. Those results meant that I needed to think from scratch about my most basic assumptions about my personal and professional lives. Eventually that meant building a new life.

If you go into politics, you are inviting heat, because the stakes are high. But the scrutiny increasingly applies to your family, not just to you. And the Labour leadership election was a campaign with a unique dynamic. Everything had an additional and unwelcome edge. All sorts of things suddenly couldn't be said, because in the media cacophony a political difference would be blown up into a family feud. That remains the case today.

All of my learning had been about the need to focus politics on the country's voters. I ran for the leadership because I thought I had ideas and skills to make Labour a force for change again, able to bring positive change to people's lives. But political parties can become focused on themselves, debating in their own goldfish bowl, separated from a majority of the public rather than representing them. After thirteen years in government, there was an easy market in railing against the compromises of office—which was much easier than putting them right. When that happens, a political party becomes a pressure group standing outside the corridors of power, not a party of government commanding them. That happened to Labour after 2010.

Government and politics are two sides of the same coin. They have common demands but also distinctive elements. And you can't have one without the other. I enjoy campaigning and in the leadership campaign was enthused and inspired by a community organizing movement I started (Movement for Change). But I was probably better at government than at politics—the balance of action and persuasion, the bigger picture over the narrowly partisan view, the policy over the personality. Certainly I was better at the business of government focused on the country than the dynamics of politics within the party. And I didn't make the shift from a mentality of governing to a mentality of campaigning fast enough.

After the 2010 leadership election, my party was out of power, and I was out of power in my party. I wanted Ed to beat the Conservatives but thought he chose the wrong track to do so. My choice was silence or division. I didn't want either. I was in my prime professional years but felt I was going through the motions. The Conservative-Liberal coalition government did not listen to my ideas on youth unemployment, on which I led an independent commission. My party had chosen an alternative course, and anything I said was construed as a bitter attack on my brother, with the substance of my point obscured by alleged psychodrama. I felt I wasn't achieving anything. I needed to find a way to break out.

NGO Leader

My chance would come in July 2012. I was having lunch with my friend and former Cabinet colleague James Purnell. I was a frustrated MP; he was a filmmaker. We had both served in Labour governments and were convinced that Labour was now a long way from government and heading further away. We both thought the Conservatives would win again. We were discussing career choices.

James asked whether I had heard that the International Rescue Committee was looking for a new CEO. The truth is that not only did I not know the job was open, but I had only a hazy idea of what the IRC was. James said it was a humanitarian organization based in New York. I sensed for the first time that there might be a way to work on something I believed in without the constraints and baggage of my position in British politics. I immediately visited the organization's website. The values of the organization were potent, but its impact was not clear. In that gap I saw an opportunity to make a real difference to something that mattered.

Nine months and three interviews later, I was walking into a conference room opposite Grand Central Terminal in New York to address the three hundred or so staff then based at the IRC headquarters. My family was with me that day, and the presence of our children made the atmosphere warm rather than wary. It was a new start. I told the staff why I had applied for the job: the significance of the humanitarian challenge, the potential of the IRC, and my family story. I said that if the IRC did not exist, it would need to be invented: the needs were so great that the world required an organization whose driving focus and expertise was the lives of displaced people.

I was very conscious that I was not from the humanitarian sector and guessed that some of my new colleagues would be, too. I tried to explain how my previous life as a politician had prepared me for my new one—not just my knowledge of public policy and foreign countries but the combination of idealism and pragmatism I had developed along the way. I thought I could apply some of my lessons from politics: how to honor expertise by learning from it, how to use a fresh pair of eyes to establish vision and strategy, how the sweet spot in a contro-versy can give definition to a project or cause, how to rally support and build coalitions.

The people I have met—staff, volunteers, the people we serve—have both educated and inspired me. Their stories are in this book. The aid workers who turned the chaos, resig-nation, and danger of eight hundred tired and fearful refugees stranded in Lesvos, Greece, on a Sunday evening in September 2015, 40 kilometers (25 miles) from the registration center, into an orderly sequence of bus journeys that prioritized the old, the sick, and the very young. The pastoralist farmer in Ethiopia who told me, "Water is life, and you have given us life." Those people have helped change me. I still get excited by statistics, but it is the human stories that are inspiring.

I set out here what I have learned and what can be done—by governments, businesses, and individuals. If this crisis is to be tackled successfully, we all have to play our part. I don't just want to convey what governments should do; I also want you to feel a sense of urgency and a sense of agency—the urge to do something and the tools to do so. Because I know that it was the decisions of individual citizens that saved the lives of my relatives eighty years ago, and that same spirit is what's needed today.

Children play in the Nyarugusu refugee camp in Tanzania.

1 The Crisis

Before I took up my post as IRC president in September 2013, I wanted to get a sense of the conditions facing refugees and displaced people around the world and the work of the organization to address their needs. I had read about tens of millions of people displaced by war and persecution, but what were their lives really like? It turned out that there was a jarring mismatch between some of the assumptions that I brought into the job and the realities of the situation on the ground.

I went to Jordan in May 2013 and Kenya in July of that year. Each country was hosting around 600,000 registered refugees, and in Jordan the government said there were an equal number unregistered. I had in my mind the iconic image of a refugee: someone in a refugee camp, standing behind wire.

In Jordan I was taken to the Za'atari refugee camp, then home to 120,000 people. At the time it was in a state of some chaos. The camp management was worried about building plans gone awry, criminal networks running amok, and lack of coordination in health care and education services. But the real eye-opener was not in the camp; it was in the town of Mafraq, 20 kilometers (13 miles) away from Za'atari.

In 2011, Mafraq had had 120,000 residents. With the arrival of Syrian refugees, the population had doubled in the space of a few months. Everything was overflowing with people, from streets to schools to shops.

My first visit to the back room of the IRC health center in Mafraq is etched on my memory. It was next door to a room used for child care. The corridors of the center were dominated by the hubbub of patients waiting to see doctors. The majority of people, most of them sitting on chairs, were mothers with children. Above their heads were notices explaining the importance of hand washing and some posters from the US and UK governments, which were funding the center.

In the back, the atmosphere was different. There were thirty women and girls in a bare room, sitting on the floor with their backs to the walls. There were a couple of tables with water and tissues. By word of mouth they had found out that this was a space where women could come together safely and talk, cry, plan, and even dream. All present wore head scarves, usually solid colors, often bright pink, orange, or blue but sometimes black. It was hot, and I noticed that some women, despite the heat, were wearing thick robes, almost drapery-weight material, which presumably had come with them from Syria.

Some averted their eyes from me. Others were intrigued. The only time they smiled was when I asked if they thought they would ever go home to Syria. "Inshallah" (God willing), they said in unison. They talked about how there were school places for some of the girls, but they would not let them go because they were scared that they would not be safe on the route. They said they were running down their savings to pay the rent. They explained that their husbands and sons worked in the informal economy, dodging the Jordanian authorities. They talked about the houses, relatives, and lives they had left behind.

Those were urban refugees. Far from being the exception, they are the majority, not just in Jordan but around the world. Of the 25 million people (refugees and asylum seekers) who have fled across borders from war and persecution, only around 4 million are in organized refugee camps, mainly in sub-Saharan Africa.[1] The biggest camps are cities in themselves—in the case of Za'atari, at the time it was the fourth-biggest city in Jordan. But 60 percent of all refugees live in urban areas, not camps.[2]

This matters because the needs of people in urban areas are different from those in camps. Shelter is not given to them. Food is not distributed to them. Education, health care, and other systems of support need to be designed to fit in with the local community.

Long-term Displacement

The assumption that the majority of refugees live in camps as opposed to urban areas is not the only mismatch between perception and reality. When I began my work at the IRC, I had assumed that most refugees and displaced people were homeless for a few years and then went home. Then I started talking to refugees.

When I went to what was then the world's largest refugee camp, Dadaab, in eastern Kenya, I got a lesson in what long-term displacement means. The clue was in the name: *dadaab*, in the local dialect, means "rocky hard place."

The camp was built in 1992–3 as a temporary shelter for Somalis seeking safety in the face of the terrible civil war ravaging their country. More than twenty years later, I met Silo, a young woman living in the camp.

She lived in a relatively peaceful area of the camp. Her home was fenced in by strips of thorny wood. (A book about Dadaab by Ben Rawlence is entitled *City of Thorns* because of the prevalence of the brush.) Silo's dwelling was a round structure only a few meters in diameter. It was made of wood, tenting, rags, cardboard. The tin door appeared to have been made from reused food containers. She had two children, one of whom wore a much-used red T-shirt with OBAMA printed on it in black letters.

The real surprise came when I asked her whether she thought she would ever go home to Somalia. "What do you mean, go home?" she replied. "I was born here." When I followed up with the camp management, they told me that of the 330,000 Somalis then living in the camp, 100,000 had been born there.

I shouldn't have been shocked. When I visited a Burmese refugee camp in the Mae Sot district of Thailand, I met the camp committee, Burmese refugees who helped represent the residents to management. The secretary was a very articulate man in his early thirties. He was smartly turned out, educated, efficient. When I asked whether he could conceive of ever going back to Burma (Myanmar), he patiently explained that he had never lived in the country because his parents had fled to the camp in Thailand before he was born.

The global figures are complicated, but the basic point is clear: displacement as a result of conflict or persecution is long term, not short term. Recent data show that the average refugee displacement (not just in camps) is ten years and that after a person has been a refugee for five years, the average duration of displacement is twenty-one years.[3]

One reason is that wars within states tend to last longer than wars between them. David Armitage shows in his book *Civil Wars: A History in Ideas* that these wars tended to last three times longer in the second half of the twentieth century than in the first half—and are much more prone to recur than any others. Armitage reminds us of Paul Collier's insight: "The most likely legacy of a civil war is further civil war."[4]

The Lebanese civil war lasted fifteen years, from 1975 to 1990, but in the end the warring parties agreed to share power rather than fight over it. The wars in Sierra Leone, Liberia, and East Timor have ended, in some cases with extensive outside intervention. But the evidence is that the bloodletting of war poisons the prospects for and stability of peace. If you look at

Afghanistan, where civil war has dominated for most of the last forty years, you can see the danger. Somalia and DRC have also seen civil wars stretch across generations.

This matters because if people are displaced from their homes for ten years rather than just ten weeks or ten months, their needs change. Their kids will be desperate for education. They themselves will need work. The countries supporting them will need more help.

Hosts and Sources

You might guess from the Western media—British coverage of the so-called jungle refugee settlement in Calais, France, or American reporting of the debate about Syrian refugee entry into the United States—that most refugees are in Western countries. That is wrong. Badly wrong. Another assumption comes face-to-face with reality.

Together the top ten refugee-hosting countries account for only 2.5 percent of global income.[5] They are poor or at best middle-income countries. Turkey has 2.9 million registered refugees; Pakistan, 1.4 million; Lebanon, 1 million; Iran and Uganda, around 1 million apiece; Ethiopia, 0.8 million; and so on.[6] In Lebanon one in four people is a refugee from Syria, Palestine, or Iraq.[7]

This is the reality of the global refugee crisis today: it is concentrated in the poorer parts of the world. Europe, accounting for more than 20 percent of global income, has 11 percent of the world's refugees. The United States, with

25 percent of global income, has 1 percent of the world's refugees.[8]

When you stop and think, it stands to reason that most refugees are not in the West. The large majority of them stop in a country neighboring the one from which they fled. In addition to more than 5 million Palestinians, around 13.5 million refugees (nearly 80 percent) come from ten countries far from the Western world: Syria, Afghanistan, South Sudan, Somalia, Sudan, DRC, Central African Republic, Myanmar, Eritrea, and Burundi.

There are also 40 million internally displaced people (IDPs) as a result of conflict or persecution. Last year one new IDP was created every second.[9] Nicholas Burns, formerly undersecretary in the US State Department, calls those people "On the Runs," to try to get away from the bureaucratese of terms such as IDP. These people remain within their home country but have fled from their homes because of conflict or persecution. The vast majority, like refugees, are nowhere near rich countries.

Since so many displaced people are homeless for a long time, live in urban areas, not camps, and are concentrated in countries that are poor or middle income, there is a fourth challenge to the prevailing assumptions. Though it is traditional to see the drive against poverty, so-called development, as separate from the humanitarian work of responding to crisis, the reality is that today's refugees and displaced people are the new global poor.

Displacement and Poverty

Laurence Chandy and his research colleagues at the Brookings Institution have catalogued the extraordinary reductions in extreme poverty over the past twenty-five years. According to the World Bank, extreme poverty is now defined as an income of less than $1.90 a day.[10] The proportion of people in extreme poverty was reduced from 55 percent in 1950 to one in ten in 2013 (the most recent year with good data).[11] That is still over 750 million people—a scar in a world more than fifty times as rich as in the 1950s.[12] But rapid progress nonetheless.

The composition of this poverty, however, has shifted significantly toward countries affected by conflict. Economic growth, albeit unequally distributed, is reducing poverty in states where there is peace. Think of China and India, where hundreds of millions of people have been taken out of extreme poverty in the last thirty years and a middle class, also of hundreds of millions, has been built.

But in countries where there is conflict, development is set back and poverty is the result. So although the global extreme poverty rate fell from 37 percent to 16 percent from 1990 to 2010, conflict sends the process into reverse. Chandy and his colleagues cite the example of Ivory Coast: the poverty rate has gone from 10 percent in the late 1980s to 35 percent as a result of unrest, military coups, and civil wars.[13] Their summary of the global situation is worth quoting: "It should come as no surprise that conflict is a dominant feature among the countries that are losing the battle against extreme poverty. . . . Global poverty is becoming more concentrated in these countries: in 1990, one in five poor people in the world lived in a fragile state; two in five do so today." Predictions for 2030 suggest that the figure could reach two-thirds.[14]

Of the thirty-one countries in the World Bank classification of low income, twenty-seven are fragile states suffering from political, security, or environmental weakness.[15] It is a vicious cycle: war and poverty go together with refugee flows, which produce more fragility and more refugees, who themselves are increasingly poor as the duration of their displacement lengthens. A recent World Bank–UNHCR study of Syrian refugees, among the better-off refugees in the world, found poverty rates of 60 to 70 percent.[16] The study noted that "Syrian refugees living in Jordan and Lebanon have experienced shock after shock, pushing them into destitution."

So the "refugee crisis" has the following components: record numbers of people are fleeing violence; they are displaced for longer than ever before; they are concentrated in a small number of countries outside the wealthy parts of the world; and they make up a growing proportion of the world's poor. There is one additional factor: climate change is not just a looming danger; it is part of today's equation.

Climate Refugees?

In 2006, I was called to see the prime minister. He was reshuffling his government and wanted to promote me. So far, so good. I went to his small study next to the Cabinet Room. We sat in armchairs, and one star of the Downing Street staff, an Irish woman named Vera who had seen it all and was not shy about offering advice, brought in cups of tea. As usual Tony Blair was friendly and purposeful: "I want you to be Secretary of State for Environment, Food, and Rural Affairs." That hadn't been part of my plan. "But I don't know one end of a cow from another!" is all I can remember saying. He thought I could learn. More important, there was a responsibility to turn our words on climate change into policy. On that he was right.

Four months later, we published in draft form the world's first long-term, legally binding emission reduction requirements. They required the United Kingdom to achieve 60 percent cuts in carbon and other emissions by 2050—later amended to 80 percent—and set into place the institutional machinery to monitor and enforce the requirement. It is the piece of legislation of which I am most proud.

I am not a scientist, but I know that if 97 percent of doctors told me I was at risk of a heart attack, I would go into hospital for a bypass. That is what I feel about climate change. The vast majority of scientists have agreed and explained, over and over again, why and how the burning of carbon is contributing to man-made change in the climate and demonstrated the data to show this is happening. The second-round effects, such as ocean acidification, only add to the dangers. The reckless, feckless, ignorant irresponsibility of those who deny the facts or don't care about them is grotesque.

In legal terms, the definition of refugees in international law does not cover people who cross borders because of climate change. Also, displacement experts such as Elizabeth Ferris make the point that climate is likely to be one factor among several contributing to decisions to move.[17] Yet when I talk to some of the people displaced in Africa, they tell me that climate change is happening and that it is affecting their lives *now*.

Abdullahi Mohammed is the Ethiopian farmer who told me that the IRC's water project had given him and his community life. I met him on the bare, hot land in the east of the country. Dressed in a T-shirt, checked shirt, and multi-colored robe, he carried a walking stick and had a limp. At forty-nine, younger than me, he looked closer to sixty. He told me he had had nine children, three of whom had died.

Abdullahi Mohammed was the chairman of the local committee that would manage the water system built by the IRC staff. It was important that there be some charge for the water, to ensure that people did not waste it and to pay for the upkeep of the system. He told me that he had learned from his grandfather about the conditions on the land and that his land was changing—becoming hotter and drier. Before the water project, he explained, he and his cattle had been forced to travel twelve hours for water. Life was becoming more and more fragile, making a livelihood an increasingly difficult struggle.

The potential for long-term drying trends, rising sea levels, and glacier melt (with the impact on river flow) to affect human movements is clear. But there is not good data on how long-term changes in, for example, the reduced fertility of land because of drought have affected the movement of people. What we do know is that the changing climate is not just a matter of higher temperatures; it is also a matter of more extreme weather events. And we do have evidence of the impact of those.

In 2016, more than 24 million people were internally displaced due to natural disasters.[18] Eighty-six percent were the result of weather-related hazards: floods, storms, fires. The rest were geophysical (for example, earthquakes). Not all of those disasters can be pinned at the door of climate change. But given the compelling science about the danger of more extreme weather events, the potential for their impact on displacement is clear.

There is also a further pressure worth considering: the role of climate change as a driver of conflict, which in turn drives displacement. Former UN secretary-general Ban Ki-moon said, "Amid the diverse social and political causes, the Darfur conflict began as an ecological crisis, arising at least in part from climate change."[19] What he meant was that the conflict in Darfur in western Sudan is in part a conflict over resources that are becoming increasingly scarce because of climate change. Similarly, studies of the Syria conflict have pointed to the 2008–2012 drought in the northeast of the country, the resultant flight of farmers and herders from the land to the cities, and the contribution of that frustrated group to the explosion of anger in the country.[20]

A recent briefing for the G20 (the group of the twenty richest economies) concluded that conflict can be induced or aggravated by climate change.[21] That makes sense. So although there might not (yet) be groups of people who can be labeled "climate refugees," there is likely to be increased pressure on population movements by changes in the climate.

Refugees and Migrants

The faulty assumptions about refugees, however mistaken, come from somewhere real. They reflect another world: that of Europe after the Second World War, when the laws and practices underpinning the current humanitarian system were established.

By the war's end in May 1945, cities had been destroyed, governments overrun, borders redrawn, and many millions of soldiers and civilians killed. More than 40 million refugees were spread across Europe. By 1947, after mass returns, there were still 7 million people in resettlement camps for displaced people.[22]

It was clear that the world had to establish rights for civilians who had been caught up in the war. That effort began with the 1948 Universal Declaration of Human Rights, which recognized the right of people to seek asylum from persecution. In 1951, the UN Refugee Convention was ratified, creating a legal definition of a refugee, and a high commission (United Nations High Commission for Refugees) was established to care for them.

The convention defined a refugee as someone who is outside his or her country of nationality due to a "well-founded fear of being persecuted for reasons of race, religion, nationality, membership of a particular social group or political opinion."[23] With refugee status came rights, above all the right not to be forced to return to a country in which there is risk of serious harm (so-called nonrefoulement), and also minimum standards of treatment, such as access to the courts and primary education. Adjudication of refugee status would be determined by the UNHCR or a responsible state. Court judgments and UNHCR practice have broadened the definition over the years. The key point is that refugees are people who cannot safely go home.

The original convention was meant to be temporary, until people returned to their homes.[24] And it was limited to Europe, reflecting a myopia about the refugee problem. Only in 1967 was the convention's mandate extended to establish universal coverage for the rights drawn up in 1951. Today 148 states are party to the convention or the 1967 Protocol Relating to the Status of Refugees (142 have signed both).[25]

Built into the definition of a refugee in the UN convention is another tension between perception and reality, concerning the relationships between refugees and economic migrants.

Economic migrants are people who choose to move to improve their standard of living. But in many quarters, the distinction between forced and voluntary displacement, political versus economic, is unclear.

In addition to the 65 million forcibly displaced (refugees, asylum seekers, and internally displaced people), 220 million people have left their home country seeking, among other things, economic improvement; 750 million people are on the move within their own country for predominantly economic reasons.[26] The truth is that the dividing line between political and economic reasons for migration is blurred.

When I went to Lesvos, Greece, in 2015 and drove to the north of the island to meet people arriving across the Aegean Sea from Turkey, there was a steady stream of people walking in the opposite direction, toward the UNHCR reception center 40 kilometers (25 miles) away. Many were Syrian. Some were Afghan. I also met young Moroccans and Algerians, whose motive, they told me, was fundamentally economic. And then there are people who start as economic migrants but who are robbed, beaten, even enslaved, adding complexity to the adjudication of their status.

"Mixed migration," a category that includes some who are fleeing for economic reasons and some for political reasons, is a feature of the modern world. It is also the case that war, poverty, and climate change can come together to propel people to flee. So the distinction between the people who are forced across borders and those who choose to cross them is not as neat and tidy as the framers of the original refugee convention might have hoped.

Nonetheless, I think it is important to try to maintain the distinctive status of refugees. The rights of refugees are founded on the idea that they are in a different position from people who choose to emigrate.

The family bombed from their home in Aleppo, the girls facing violence for seeking education in northeast Nigeria, the religious minority persecuted for their beliefs, the political dissident in fear of his or her life face a different set of incentives from the student seeking better economic opportunity or the family opting to join cousins in a new country to improve their life chances. They should have greater rights and protections, because they face far graver threats to life and limb. Gray areas should not be an excuse to dilute rights.

The tactical reason to defend the integrity and distinction of refugee status is that, with 245 million people in total on the move across borders, there is no way that the particular needs of those fleeing war and persecution will be recognized if they are grouped together with those who are seeking to improve their economic circumstances. Conflation of the needs of refugees and immigrants is dangerous for the politics of both issues.

The Challenge

The rising tide of people forced to leave their homes because of conflict or persecution is one of the most challenging issues facing the world today. But the policy challenge is about more than its size; it is also about its nature. And the global community is struggling to catch up with that new reality.

Half of refugee children of primary school age are not in school.[27] The vast majority of refugees are living in poverty.[28] Half of the world's unsafe abortions take place in conditions of war and displacement.[29] And the gap between need and support is growing.[30]

This matters in and of itself. These lives are being blighted by abuse and neglect. But I have learned over the last four years that although humanitarian need is the product of political crisis, unmet humanitarian need is a cause of political instability. In other words, the line of causality does not only run from failed politics to humanitarian crisis; it also runs in the opposite direction, from insufficient or ineffective humanitarian action to political instability.

Politics in Europe in the last few years is testimony to that. The Syrian refugee crisis was not recognized as a European issue until it was too late. In the United States, the failure to agree on immigration reform and address the issue of undocumented migrants has boiled over into furious attacks on refugees and migrants. In Kenya, elections have been affected by security concerns about Somali refugees. Pakistan has returned half a million Afghans to their country—many of them against their will, many of them entering Afghanistan for the first time. King Abdullah of Jordan says his country is at the "boiling point."[31]

We know from history that when it comes to refugees, politics and policy are never far apart. The most inspiring advances have shaped as well as reflected national and international mood. Leadership really matters. For example, Eleanor Roosevelt, the widow of President Franklin D. Roosevelt, played an instrumental role in the adoption of the UN Universal Declaration of Human Rights in 1948. It included the right to "seek and enjoy" asylum from persecution.[32] Maybe Mrs. Roosevelt was reflecting on the dark period of US history during the Second World War.

In July 1941, Albert Einstein, ten months a US citizen, was hearing about the planning by the Nazis of the "Final Solution" that would seek to exterminate European Jewry. In desperation he wrote to Eleanor Roosevelt from his retreat at Lake Saranac in upstate New York to register "deep concern" at the policies of her husband's administration. A "wall of bureaucratic measures" erected by the State Department, "alleged to be necessary to protect America against subversive, dangerous elements," had, he wrote, made "it all but impossible to give refuge in America to many worthy persons who are the victims of Fascist cruelty in Europe."[33]

Einstein asked the first lady to raise this "truly grave injustice" with the president, but his appeal had limited effect. Paranoia that refugees would, if granted entry to the United

States, turn on their host and spy for its enemies persisted. The annihilation the following year of some 2.7 million Jews— nearly half of all Jewish victims of the Holocaust—could not dispel that prejudice. Nor did the killing in 1942 result—amid economic depression, the battle against the Axis, and strains of popular and political xenophobia—in a US response to the refugees' plight. Sixty-one percent of Americans did not even want to let 10,000 refugee children enter the United States.[34] The US "wall" against refugees would remain largely standing until the beginning of 1944, the year before the Allied victory.

The crisis, then, was not just a crisis of policy; it was also a crisis of politics. That is also the case today. It is incumbent on us all to decide what personal responsibility we are willing to take in addressing this refugee crisis. In short, what has it got to do with us?

2 Why We Should Care

Walls in people's heads are sometimes more durable than walls made of concrete blocks.

—Willy Brandt, mayor of Berlin, 1957–1966;
chancellor of West Germany, 1969–1974

The injunction to love a stranger is as old as the Bible. So it is fitting that Pope Francis has emerged as the most consistent, passionate, effective advocate for the world's displaced people. In 2013, he went to the island of Lampedusa, off the coast of Italy, and called out neglect of refugees as evidence of "the globalization of indifference"—a haunting and brilliant phrase that challenges all of us. In 2015, he went before the US Congress and declared in respect of the refugee crisis, "We must not be taken aback by their numbers, but rather view them as persons, seeing their faces and listening to their stories.... We need to avoid a common temptation nowadays: to discard whatever proves troublesome."[1] In 2016, when he visited the

Moria camp on the Greek island of Lesvos, he took back twelve Syrian refugees from three families, including six children, to live in Rome.[2]

The pope is not alone among faith leaders. Justin Welby, the archbishop of Canterbury, has said of the refugee crisis, "As Christians we believe we are called to break down barriers, to welcome the stranger and love them as ourselves (Leviticus 19:34), and to seek the peace and justice of our God, in our world, today."[3] Ed Stetzer, who holds the Billy Graham Chair at evangelical Wheaton College, has said, "God's people should be the first ones to open their arms to refugees."[4]

The former UK chief rabbi Jonathan Sacks has addressed the fact that religion binds people within a group but not necessarily beyond it. He wrote, "A humanitarian as opposed to a group ethic requires the most difficult of all imaginative exercises: role reversal—putting yourself in the place of those you despise, or pity, or simply do not understand."[5] Sacks's argument is that this is the radicalism of the Genesis narratives: that those outside the covenant are also blessed and must be loved. He wrote, "The people of the covenant will be strangers at home, so that they are able to make strangers feel at home. Only thus can they defeat the most powerful of all drives to evil: the sense of being threatened by the Other, the one not like me."

Dr. Omid Safi, the director of Duke University's Islamic Studies Center, has written, ". . . the Qur'an tell[s] us to treat strangers and refugees with kindness and tenderness because we ourselves were once strangers."[6]

These statements of commitment and morality stand against the volleys of denigration and abuse. But you don't need to be a religious person—I am not—to make the case for support for refugees.

Values and Character

One of the family stories I was told as a child has stuck with me as both a challenge and an inspiration: a challenge because it asks what I would have done in a similar situation; an inspiration because it reveals the best of human nature.

In 1942, when my father's mother and sister were living in Brussels, they received a summons from the occupying German authorities to undergo registration. The venue was to be the main railway station. Immediately my grandmother thought something was amiss—and of course feared being transported to a concentration camp. Though some of her friends and relatives told her that it was dangerous to refuse to obey instructions, she felt it was far more dangerous to do as she was told.

So she packed her bags and made her way with her daughter (my aunt) to a small village south of Brussels where she had previously spent holidays. When she arrived at the house of one of the local Catholic farmers, Mr. Maurice, she asked him to take her in. For the rest of the war, at enormous risk to himself and his family, Mr. Maurice hid those strangers. He would have been shot on the spot if his secret had been discovered—especially since by the end of the war seventeen other Jews were also in hiding in his village.

As a teenager I asked my aunt to take me to visit him. My memory is that the farmhouse was on the edge of the village, surrounded by fields and old trees. My aunt was proud of Mr. Maurice—she was almost an extra daughter for him—and I could see why. He was by then in his seventies, with white hair carefully parted. He was smartly dressed and fortunately spoke in soft, slow French that even with my schoolboy learning I could follow.

We talked about family, memories, hopes. But there was something I wanted to know. I feared it was naive, possibly even insulting, but I needed to know: Why had he done it? Why had he taken such a risk for the sake of my family? His answer will always stick with me. "On doit," he said. One must. It was innate in him, part of his being to help someone in trouble.

People often say that charity should begin at home. I understand that feeling. But that doesn't mean charity should end at home. Define someone whom you don't know as your brother or sister, and you set out one definition of human responsibility and kinship; define them as "other," and you set out on a different and far less humane course.

Two of the most basic human values, without which there is no humanity, are empathy and its cousin altruism. Empathy for other people simply because they are people, not because of their race, religion, or politics, is a basic building block of what makes civilization. Just as we admire people who do great things and disdain those who do bad things, so we empathize with people in need. Or we should. In fact, the latest research shows that when we see other people in pain, it triggers the same part of our brain as when we are in pain ourselves. That would mean that the question of our response to the pain of others is a matter of whether we live up to what is in our DNA. Show empathy for those we do not know, turn that empathy into action, and we live out the most basic value of humankind. Fail, and we show that we have no moral compass at all.

In his 1986 Nobel Peace Prize speech, Holocaust survivor Elie Wiesel added a further point. He said that victims of political repression depend on the way we use our freedom to make a difference for them. They need us to use our freedom, and our power, to speak and act for them. But he added that "the quality of our freedom depends on theirs." In other words, our own freedom is depleted by the suffering of others. It is a version of John Donne's line "No man is an island." When someone else suffers, we all lose.

This is especially so when the needs of others are the result of external force, not personal failing. By legal definition, refugees are in need through no fault of their own. They are victims of persecution or war.

The old excuse for ignoring their plight was that we could not know what was happening on the other side of the world.

In our ignorance we could not be held responsible for their suffering. That was one reason Americans were given for keeping their doors shut to European Jews in the 1930s and early 1940s. As a result many were killed when they could have been saved.

Refugees are a hard case. They come from very different countries, so they are strangers, not neighbors. Yet today we know more about victims of war than at any other time in history. Ignorance is no excuse when it comes to people fleeing from Aleppo, Syria; Nyal, South Sudan; or Rakhine state, Myanmar. Today their plight can be seen at any moment in the palms of our hands.

Because they are a hard case, refugees are a good test—of us. Our response reveals whether we live up to the most basic of human values. To me that would be reason enough for addressing the refugee crisis. But it cannot be the end of the story.

Western countries, by virtue of their history, wealth, power, and values, have a distinctive set of reasons for helping refugees and displaced people. That point was summed up very eloquently in testimony to Congress from the then US secretary of health, education, and welfare, Joseph Califano, in 1979. Congress was considering legislation to put into domestic law the contents of the 1951 UN Convention on Refugees and the 1967 protocol to that convention. Secretary Califano said, "There are relatively few moments in our national life when . . . what we choose to do about a political problem expresses what we really are as a nation. . . . And the issue of refugees now seeking haven in America brings us precisely such a moment. By our choice on this issue, we will reveal to the world—and more importantly to ourselves—whether we truly live by our ideals, or simply carve them in monuments."[7]

This is the moral call to arms at the core of the refugee crisis. It applies to all countries and cultures. But it is also a call to a particular understanding of US history and responsibility. Without a doubt the refugee crisis is a global crisis that needs a global response. But I also believe that Western countries, because of their history, values, and interests, have a special responsibility to lead that response.

History and the "West"

I recognize immediately that the notion of a singular "West" or "Western world" can be problematic. It neglects the North/South divide. It can sound exclusivist or supremacist—or bossy and self-preening.

That was the view that animated the long-serving, extremely smart, hard-bitten Russian foreign minister, Sergey Lavrov, in my conversations with him. Things got off to a difficult start when, in my first week as foreign secretary, I had to expel eight Russian diplomats from London in retaliation for the refusal of the Russians to cooperate in bringing to justice the killers of Alexander Litvinenko in London. We tried to make a serious point without ending the whole relationship. The Russians, led by Lavrov, replied in kind, expelling eight British diplomats from Moscow.

To Lavrov, nothing about Western foreign policy had integrity because it was all founded, in his mind, on double-talk. When I challenged him about the Russian invasion of Georgia in 2008, he would bring up Iraq (as well as screaming down the phone that the president of Georgia was a "f***ing lunatic"). When I argued about the Sri Lankan bombing of Tamil civilians in the Jaffna Peninsula in 2009, he would remind me that his first diplomatic posting had been in Sri Lanka and that he was a fluent Sinhalese speaker, and then he would bring up the bombing of the Chinese Embassy by NATO forces in Belgrade in 1998.

Western countries should not preen themselves on their moral virtue; we have plenty of mistakes to apologize for. But for me the notion of the West as a political entity also has an inspiring and inclusive history and meaning.

A key date is 1941, when the Atlantic Charter was signed by President Roosevelt and Prime Minister Winston Churchill in Newfoundland. The United States would not formally enter the war for four more months (though it was increasingly believed that it would), but the meeting was about planning for postwar peace.

Former German foreign minister Joschka Fischer calls the Atlantic Charter the "birth certificate" of the West.[8] The charter eschewed territorial gains for the Allied powers. In fact, in commitments to national self-determination, it foreshadowed wide-ranging decolonization in Africa and elsewhere. But the charter above all focused on a postwar world of interdependence and international cooperation, founded on international law and mutual respect and committed to the idea that order as well as justice depended on a firm foundation in values that are the property of no one but should be the birthright of all. The animating insight was that the world could not afford to repeat the mistakes of the shallow and punitive peace after World War I, and it was the job of the richest and most powerful countries in the world to lead the process of building a stable, legitimate global system.

The writer and historian Ian Buruma has summarized the significance of the charter thus: "The words of the Atlantic Charter, drawn up by Churchill and Roosevelt in 1941, resonated deeply throughout a war-torn Europe: Trade barriers would be lowered, peoples would be free, social welfare would advance and global cooperation would ensue. Churchill called the charter 'not a law, but a star.'"[9]

Out of the Atlantic Charter sprang the political and economic institutions and norms of the postwar world: the United Nations, the International Monetary Fund, the World Bank, the General Agreement on Tariffs and Trade (forerunner of the World Trade Organization). In fact, the precursor of the UN Charter was based on the principles of the Atlantic Charter.

Crucially, there was a commitment not just to new insti-tutions but also to accompanying laws and practices, which took concrete form in the UN Universal Declaration on Human Rights, international humanitarian law, and the UN Convention on Refugees.

For centuries refugees were not counted and did not count. They were seen as the unfortunate collateral of the competition for global power. But in the period after World War II, they and their rights were finally recognized in law. The current international refugee protection regime was written by the Western world after the Second World War; was underwritten by every Western democratic country; and eventually moved beyond the West—to universal declarations of rights and universal aspirations for standards of protection for refugees.

So when it comes to the response to the refugee crisis, there is good cause to honor the history that led Western nations to found a global order in a way that afforded protections to victims of war. The hard-won gains for refugees after World War II represent a high point of moral leadership in Western countries and should be recognized and celebrated as such. Trash the protections for refugees, and we trash our own history of global leadership.

That is not all. The UN institutions and laws brought together a range of countries: democracies and autocracies, capitalists and communists. But the nations of the democratic West made a distinctive claim: that freedoms of the individual regarding thought, religion, and conscience constituted fundamental human rights that should be respected the world over. That commitment is tested in our treatment of refugees.

Democracy and Pluralism

The nationalist, populist movements that have sprung
up in the last twenty years, such as UKIP in the United
Kingdom, the National Front in France, and the Tea Party
in the United States, take aim at the institutions, norms, and
values of the postwar order. They argue that the economic
bargain of free trade is unfair and that international political
institutions are undemocratic. But the greatest passion of
their adherents is animus toward refugees and immigrants,
especially Muslims.

Their sentiments are vengeful, demonizing, and dehuman-
izing. President Trump talked about Syrian refugees as "one
of the great Trojan horses."[10] Marine Le Pen talked of Muslim
"occupation" of France.[11] The Netherlands' Geert Wilders
talked about an Islamic invasion of Europe.[12]

This is a far cry from George Washington's proclamation
more than two hundred years ago that "the bosom of America
is open to receive not only the opulent & respectable Stranger,
but the oppressed & persecuted of all Nations & Religions."[13]
For refugees fleeing for freedom, Western countries have
been a source of hope and a place of haven. When people
have been persecuted by their own government because of
their political views or religion, they have turned to Western
countries for refuge. And by definition Western countries
have helped define their place in the world by offering safety
for those fleeing societies where pluralism is seen as a threat
to the country, not a feature of the society. By doing so we

have not shown ourselves to be suckers; we have shown our strength, not our weakness.

When Western countries accept the claim of refugees to start a new life, they assert a set of beliefs about the dignity, even sanctity, of the individual and the importance of pluralism in society. Welcoming refugees from behind the Iron Curtain during the Cold War was a judgment on communism. Protecting refugees from Myanmar is a statement that discrimination against minorities is unacceptable. Sheltering refugees from Syria means condemning the bombing tactics of Bashar al-Assad.

Cubans, Russians, Chinese, Afghans, Burmese, Iranians, and Eritreans have all sought protection in the West on the grounds of politics or religion. If we won't accept them, we compromise on the very values that underpin our nations. We tell the world that we stand for nothing. And we say to those living under oppression that they are on their own.

That is one reason the proposal of the Trump administration to privilege refugee status for Christian refugees, in the January 2017 version of its executive order restricting immigrant and refugee entry into the United States, was so egregious. It violated the facts—because religious persecution, of any group, is already grounds for refugee status. And it put religious persecution above political persecution, when all the lessons of Western history teach us that there is a premium on protecting all those who are persecuted, whatever the reason, and promoting the rights of individuals to make their own choices, whatever their religion and their politics.

The freedom of the individual and his or her ability to write their own story, irrespective of race, religion, gender, or sexuality, is the core idea that distinguishes free societies from dictatorships. And when free societies abandon their commitment to provide a haven from dictatorship, they cede ground to a relativism that is not just demeaning but dangerous.

Foreign Policy: You Break It, You Try to Mend It

Support for refugees is not only about high ideals and global leadership. One of the complex challenges for countries in this crisis centers around responsibility. Issues of whether and how to support refugees ask whether countries are ready to address the consequences of their foreign policy mistakes. In the United States, for example, the greatest number of refugees is the so-called Vietnamese boat people. Among the reasons for giving them refuge was the United States' role in the Vietnam War.

I believe it is false, even dangerous, to blame the West for all the world's problems. The biggest refugee crisis in the world today is in Syria, where the West has been conspicuously absent from the civil war. There is also a major crisis of internal displacement in northeast Nigeria. That has not been caused by Western countries. To incriminate Western capitalism for every global problem only distracts us from taking action and undermines the case when the West is really to blame.

But there are contemporary refugee crises that speak more directly to the role of Western foreign policy, most recently and most obviously in Afghanistan and in Iraq. I feel both personally.

I had just become a member of Parliament in the United Kingdom when the date 9/11 was inscribed in historical memory. That morning I was in Newcastle, near my constituency, giving a speech about the manufacturing industry in the northeast of England. I was quite buoyant as I had a slot to discuss my speech on the BBC regional lunchtime news at around 1:30 p.m. (8:30 a.m. New York time). When I eventually got into a taxi to go back to South Shields, the driver told me there was news of something "kicking off" in the United States.

When the details started coming through, I went to the house of one of my staff and watched the TV bulletins. Like everyone else, what happened that day was completely different from anything I had ever seen or known. I searched for parallels. The IRA? The PLO? No. This was something else. I felt sick for the dead and injured and their families and dread for the reckoning to follow.

Politicians are usually full of words and opinions. When I went to the emergency session of the House of Commons, I remember the quiet in the Members' Tea Room. There were hushed conversations but none of the usual hubbub.

In the wake of the attacks I supported the government's decision to declare war on the Taliban and the pledge to stop Afghanistan being used as a base for Al Qaeda. I had not visited or studied Afghanistan, but I saw no alternative but to try to reclaim lost ground. By 2005, I had just been appointed to the Cabinet when there was the first discussion about extending the campaign to Helmand province.

The phrase "There is no military solution to a civil war, only a political solution" has become a cliché because it is true. The first time I met General David Petraeus, in Baghdad, he told me, "We cannot kill our way out of this problem."

That doesn't mean military force is never needed. Sometimes it takes military effort to make political progress possible. But without a political settlement to aim for, military effort has no focus. In Afghanistan, that political settlement needed two elements. One was internal to the country: the need to engage all the tribes of Afghanistan in their incredible diversity. The fact that the 2001 peace agreement in Bonn did not do this is an enduring problem to this day. The second was regional: involving countries in the region that have for a long time viewed Afghanistan as a pawn in a larger game and whose proxies are major players inside the country.

I can honestly say that as foreign secretary I led the way internationally in making this argument.[14] I think it is relevant today, not just in Afghanistan but more broadly. But I can equally honestly say that I did not win the argument. The international military wanted to put more pressure on the Taliban before talking. The politicians didn't want to be branded as soft on terrorism. You can see the consequences today in the lackluster Western debate about how to make a sustainable difference in Afghanistan. In fact, the State Department's special Afghanistan/Pakistan team has apparently been wound up and its policy responsibility transferred to the Defense Department.

It is tempting to play "whack a mole" with the latest iteration of terrorist planning and organization, but ultimately futile. It does not get to the roots of the problem. This is the danger of the Trump administration's new policy. And although most Afghan refugees and displaced people were uprooted from their homes after the Soviet Union invaded in 1980, their continued displacement reflects the failure to achieve sufficient political buy-in to stop the fighting. Innocent civilians pay the price.

Iraq teaches some similar lessons. At the time of the decision to go to war in Iraq, in 2003, I was a minister in the Education Department. I voted to support the government's decision to participate in the war. I had read the reports on Iraq's failure to abide by the terms of the UN resolution that had concluded the 1991 Gulf War, had loyalty to the government of which I was a part, and believed in the prime minister and senior decision makers. But my assessment of the risks, and therefore my vote, was wrong, not least since there were no weapons of mass destruction found in Iraq, and that was a central point in the original rationale for the invasion. It was our—and my—biggest mistake in government. The decision to invade has turned out to be a deep and lasting error, and many Iraqis are still paying the price.

It is true that Iraq represents a case of "winning the war, losing the peace," in that the war was won relatively easily and the problems arose in the postwar administration. The decisions by the United States about how the country should be run created and exacerbated problems far beyond the imagination. To that extent there is a case that things could have turned out differently—that the decision to go to war did not necessarily doom Iraqis to all the misery they have suffered. But that is not the whole story. The decision to go to war was itself a strategic fault, since it did not take into sufficient account factors such as the impact on the power of Iran in the region. It was also a military mistake, given that the planning neglected the impact on the Afghan campaign, which was not yet, and is still not, complete.

Not all of Iraq's problems emanate from the decision to topple Saddam Hussein. He was a murderous dictator who had created more than his fair share of problems. In the Kurdish region, whose residents he viciously suppressed, today there is safety. When you visit Erbil or Sulaymaniyah, there is hope. But none of the crises facing the country is explicable without taking the invasion into account. That includes the displacement of Iraqis around the country, which now amounts to a very significant flow of people and which IRC staff are addressing as I write these words. Of course, when I visit Iraq and discuss its condition, I think about the history. There is only regret.

The Labour government had tremendous foreign policy achievements—from the massive boost to overseas aid to enlargement of the European Union to include Central Europe to humanitarian intervention in Sierra Leone and Kosovo. But as well as ruining lives in Iraq, the war poisoned center-left politics in the United Kingdom. The legacy of Iraq also hangs over the gruesome ongoing war in Syria, imprisoning policy in the mantra "Not another Iraq." So yes, I am frustrated as well as appalled by the legacy of the war.

I know humanitarian policy cannot make up for foreign policy that goes wrong. But when that happens, humanitarian policy offers one way to mitigate the consequences. Ownership lies with the countries concerned, but helping is our responsibility.

Security in a Connected World

There is a final part to the argument for the West to lead a global response to the refugee crisis. It is not the moral or historic case to care about refugees and displaced people, but instead the hardheaded strategic one.

First, the world is more interconnected than ever before. This means that instability in one part of the world ripples through to cause instability around the world. And since untended humanitarian crisis exacerbates instability, it makes strategic sense to address both the causes of refugee flows and their symptoms.

For example, the displacement crisis in northeast Nigeria matters for strategic reasons because Boko Haram is affiliated with Daesh; because destabilization of Africa's largest economy is damaging for the whole continent; because instability and ungoverned space in northeast Nigeria afflict the whole of the Lake Chad basin; and because that instability contributes to an unsustainable flow of people toward Europe.

The second element is more specific, more controversial, and more complicated. It is about relations between the West and the Muslim world. The fact is that around 60 percent of the world's refugees and asylum seekers are from Muslim-majority countries and are fleeing violence within the Muslim world.[15] This is not an easy subject to talk about, and there is great room for missteps and mistakes. But the facts are real.

The layers of the Syria crisis expose deep divisions inside the Muslim world—over the exercise of power, theology, regional and international alliances, engagement with the wider world. All are exacerbated by the growing mobility, flexibility, and ruthlessness of nonstate terrorist movements, which exploit the openness and integration of globalization to threaten those whom they deem enemies.

Of course, Afghanistan is different from Syria, and both are very different from Myanmar and the Central African Republic, where Muslim minorities suffer persecution. But the roiling turmoil within parts of the Islamic world, and the attacks on Muslims in other parts of the world, are a key part of the story of the refugee crisis and the reaction to it. Christopher de Bellaigue has written, "Islam is no settled entity. It has burst its banks and seethes with discontents and desires that are immediately recognisable as the consequence of a painful engagement with modernity."[16]

In July 2005, I was sitting in a Cabinet meeting. I was the minister for communities and local government. The mood was upbeat—London had, the day before, won the right to stage the 2012 Olympics. But toward the end of the meeting the mood turned. The transport secretary was called out to take a phone call. Then the meeting was quickly concluded, and the home secretary was asked to stay behind. We subsequently found that terrorists had struck the London transport network. Fifty-two people had been killed and more than seven hundred injured.

The attacks raised fundamental questions about intelligence production and sharing, and effective integration of Muslim minorities. Subsequent homegrown terrorism in Europe has only served to strengthen these points.

Later, as foreign secretary, I was responsible for MI6, Britain's global intelligence service, and GCHQ, the center of signals intelligence, so the interception and interruption of terrorist planning, and understanding the terrorist mind-set, were a daily concern. I spent a lot of time thinking about how the fight against international terrorism could be conducted. What would be the best way to undermine the argument of jihadists, namely that they were the only people who could adequately defend the interests and honor of Muslim populations?

The horrific terrorist attacks of recent years, even though they have in the main been "homegrown," have raised fundamental questions for Western societies: Is it possible to be both open and safe? When does pluralism become separation, separation lead to alienation, and alienation turn to violence? And what is the best way to respond to terrorist attacks and lower the chance of future ones?

From both jobs I took this lesson: Those who direct terrorist attacks in the name of Islamic purity are strategic in the way they act. Therefore, so must be the response.

The starting point is to understand, as scholar Peter Neumann explains, that jihadism by Islamist groups, even when it has a name such as Al Qaeda or proclaims itself a "caliphate" as Daesh has done, is a movement and not just an organization.[17] It is a way of thinking based on theology and ideology, not only a command structure for organizing terror.

It is important to try to understand the way tactics link to strategy for the leaders. The carnage they seek to wreak is an end in itself but also a means to a larger end, which is to provoke or further a defining, multigenerational conflict between those committed to jihad and their enemies (both Western and Islamic). So the death of the leaders and the destruction of their organization does not mean that their appeal is vanquished. That is why commentators talk about the danger of "Daesh 3.0" (and 4.0)—further iterations of thought and action, more extreme than before—even as Daesh is defeated in its citadels in Iraq and Syria.

These people find succor for their fanaticism in certain actions and statements in the West. For example, the former, now disgraced, national security advisor Michael Flynn claimed, "Fear of Muslims is *rational*."[18] In the process he confirmed the central claim of the jihadists: that religious division and conflict are inevitable.

The argument that we are doomed to a "clash of civilizations"—the name of an important book by Samuel Huntington in 1996—is in my view wrong. Part of the reason it is wrong is that violent jihadism in the name of Islam is symptomatic of a clash *within* Islam rather than between Islam and the West.

It cannot be said often enough: the majority of the victims of the appalling attacks carried out in the name of Islam are in fact Muslim. President Trump recognized this in his speech in Saudi Arabia in May 2017. More Muslims than Christians or Jews have been killed by jihadist violence because there is a clash within the Muslim world about its identity, pitting purification against pluralism.

As the Pakistani author Ahmed Rashid put it, "This is above all a war within Islam: a conflict of Sunni against Shia, but also a war by Sunni extremists against more moderate Muslims."[19] Ed Husain, a British Muslim who has made the trek from fundamentalist to counterextremist explains the divide in stark terms: "ISIS, al Qaeda and other jihadist terrorists believe in an Islam of literalism, anger, activism and political control. Most Muslims now and throughout history observed an Islam of contemplation, piety and inner goodness."[20]

In an interconnected world, all countries have a huge stake in the victory of those arguing for coexistence and pluralism within and beyond the Islamic world.[21] Western countries should be doing everything possible to enfranchise, empower, and support the vast majority of Muslims arguing against the hate being spewed by the radicals in their midst. Helping Muslim refugees, both by offering aid to countries hosting them and by welcoming vulnerable and vetted refugees to our own shores, is not just right in itself; it also plays a part in the wider effort.

A strategic effort to contribute to the fight against violent jihadism does not confuse Muslim refugees with terrorists. In fact, it recognizes that a crackdown on Muslim refugees is exactly the kind of thing that undermines the fight against terrorism. For example, former CIA director Michael Hayden has written about how President Trump's executive order on refugees will make it harder to recruit agents because "it doesn't take paranoia to connect the action of the executive order with the hateful, anti-Islamic language of the campaign," which in turn undermines the respect on which security cooperation depends.[22]

So when I say that the refugee crisis is about us, not just them, I mean that it is about basic questions of individual character and foreign policy. The humanitarian enterprise is founded on a moral claim of the victims of war—and about the empathy and altruism they are owed by the rest of us. But we should not be scared of the strategic argument. This is about the interests of nations, too. Untended humanitarian crisis is fuel for political instability. We should be committing ourselves to its management and resolution with our heads as well as our hearts.

3 The Renewal of Rescue

Kakuma
> 1. Refugee camp in Turkana province, northern Kenya.
> 2. Translation from local dialect: "Nowhere."

The question of *why* we should care for refugees is simple compared to the question of *how*. And the answer to that challenge needs dramatic redesign. Keeping people alive—life saving—is no longer enough. We need to get much better at life changing.

When I am asked whether it is depressing to work in a sector in which human misery is so present, I usually quote a filmmaker who spent time in DRC: "If you look at the statistics, you get depressed, but if you look at the people, you find hope."

It is tough to advocate for change because the humanitarian aid sector is in many ways truly remarkable. Working in the toughest conceivable circumstances, NGO and UN staff save lives, educate children, help women recover from violence, and put people to work. They do all this at growing risk to themselves, as the laws of war provide decreasing amounts of protection and the number of aid workers killed in the line of duty steadily rises.

My colleagues do humbling, inspiring, amazing work. On the front lines, they are relentlessly practical. When President Basher al-Assad gassed his own people in Khan Sheikhoun, northern Syria, IRC-supported hospitals treated some of the victims and IRC ambulance drivers got others to medical care. When famine struck in the tragically misnamed Unity State, South Sudan, an emergency team deployed to the most remote areas to offer combined health care and nutrition support. These are real heroes.

In 2016, more lives were saved and more people helped than ever before. The IRC alone reached 26 million people. More money was invested than ever before—just over $27 billion in total. Yet the gap between needs and provision grew.

Part of the answer is more funding. Money really matters. UN appeals are often only half or quarter funded. A UN special panel in 2016 reported that funding needed to be 40 percent higher overall.

In this area the United Kingdom has set a good example. The 1997 Labour manifesto promised to deliver the long-standing but long-unfulfilled UK commitment to raise aid spending to the UN target of 0.7 percent of national income. We had inherited declining aid spending but determined to increase it and to draw a clear demarcation between aid spending and military and trade interests. When I wrote that commitment in the manifesto, I couldn't imagine that twenty years later I would be explaining to American audiences that the 0.7 percent commitment had been achieved and that the United Kingdom had cross-party consensus on the issue. Those resources have saved countless lives. Between 2011 and 2015 the money has been used to reach 13 million people with emergency food assistance, immunize 67 million children, provide vital nutrition to 30 million children under the age of five and pregnant women, help 69 million people out of poverty, and support the education of 11 million children.[1] Who says government cannot make a difference? We need to see more governments around the world showing such commitment.

But the issue is not just the total spending. It is also about priorities, mind-set, and organization. Those need to change to keep up with the changing realities on the front lines. Refugees and displaced people are more likely to be displaced again than to go home, more likely to live in cities than in camps. And the majority are under the age of eighteen. Humanitarian aid has to change to reflect the new imperatives.

Think what you and I would need as refugees. Of course we would want the basics of life, such as water, sanitation, and health care. But today, education, work, and the ability to pay our own way are almost as important. We would be desperate for a sense of agency, the glimmer of hope that our actions could influence the path of our lives, the sense that we are visible, individuals in our own right, not just someone else's problem to be solved.

Too large a share of humanitarian effort still carries an imprint of the post–Second World War focus on short-term survival. This imbalance between the imperative to survive and the desire to thrive is what leads to refugee camps, set up to be temporary, ending up as permanent, and, like Kakuma in Kenya, feeling like "nowhere." And the imbalance of power between donor governments and displaced people means that the voices in Parliament or Congress matter much much more than do those in Kakuma. Accountability, which should flow downward to people in need, flows away from them and upward to donors.

Time and again when I go to the field, I hear the same thing: about power to make decisions, about economic independence, about kids and their opportunities, about the threats to women and girls. The humanitarian sector can and should respond to what refugees are telling us they need.

Give Me the Money to Make My Own Decisions

It should be obvious, but one of the things that refugees and displaced people need more than anything else is . . . money. Yet today, despite the increasing reach of global markets, only 6 percent of humanitarian aid spending is given out in the form of cash support. There are essential items to buy, in camps as well as in cities, but displaced people don't have the money to do so.

Money, in the form of vouchers, debit cards, or other secure electronic forms of support, puts power into the hands of displaced people. Rather than donors or aid agencies deciding what people need and want, they can decide for themselves. Giving money directly to those who need it empowers them to address the unique problems they face.

Put simply, nothing other than a sustained bout of successful peacemaking would have a bigger impact on the lives of the displaced than for more of the total humanitarian budget to go to cash support. That's why we are trying to distribute 25 percent of the IRC's international assistance in cash by 2020 (we are currently at 16 percent). It would be a revolution in the locus of power to the benefit of refugees and displaced people. It would also be an enormous boon to the local economies in which they live. "Why not cash?" should be the first question in any humanitarian situation.

The story of one family, from Baji in Salah ad Din province in Iraq, brings home the power of cash payments to transform humanitarian response. I visited them in Kirkuk, a city divided between Kurds and Sunnis and home to many displaced by Iraq's conflicts. The family includes a number of people with severe physical and mental disabilities.

I met them on the ground floor of an apartment block to which they had recently moved. It was a cool February day. The sky was blue, but the sun was dipping and a cool breeze was blowing through the open windows. There were no curtains and no furniture. It was going to be cold that night.

We sat on mattresses. Two young men in their twenties, part of the extended family that had been displaced together,

sat through the meeting staring straight ahead and saying
nothing (due to trauma or other illness). The disabled head
of the household, his lower limbs severely disabled, was able
to move quite fast, squatting while he talked but organizing
everyone with quick movements of his hands. A packet of
cigarettes was in his shirt pocket. His wife and daughters were
invited into the room after we had spoken. His face bore the
dark lines of hard times.

Samer, clearly the head of the household, spoke in
rapid-fire Arabic about the needs of his family. He explained
that one of his sons was outside in a wheelchair, his leg and
hip unable to move as a result of injury. His younger sons,
wearing aging Chelsea and Barcelona soccer shirts, wandered
in and out.

The family is a part of the IRC's cash payments program.
They receive 430,000 Iraqi dinars (equal to $360) each month
for three months. This money allows them to pay medical
bills, as five of the family members have disabilities and only
one is able to work. I asked them and their cousin who had
arranged the apartment rental what they did with the cash
payments. The answer was simple: "It allows us to live."

Samer made clear that displaced people know what is best
for them. Cash payments give them the power to get what they
need to survive and thrive. For them cash is king.

The IRC conducted the first study to compare refugees
who received cash with those who did not. In 2014, 87,000
refugees living in villages more than 500 meters (1,600 feet)

above sea level in Lebanon were given $575 per month via ATMs as part of a "winterization" campaign to protect them from the cold. The results were striking: the incidence of child labor went down; school attendance went up; prices did not rise; and each dollar given to the refugees generated a $2.13 increase in income in the local economy.[2]

Cash is not the answer everywhere. In some parts of the world the market economy does not function; in some conflict or disaster areas there is no possibility of a market supply of food or nonfood items, so more cash in circulation means more price inflation. But where it is appropriate, the impact is significant.

The spread of cash payments is hindered in part by inertia among donors and agencies. But there are also three serious challenges: we need to develop faster ways to identify appropriate populations and strip out time-consuming manual processes in cash distribution; we need secure financial services to be available in the places where refugees are most likely to live; and we need to reduce setup costs to maximize the amount that goes to beneficiaries.

The charity Give Directly (www.givedirectly.com) has been a pioneer in this field. It uses rigorous evidence and full transparency to show the public that their money can make a direct difference to people in need in East Africa and can also be delivered safely and efficiently.

The answer to all three challenges in the medium term is staring us in the face: ensure that all refugees are registered;

ensure that they have a unique identifier and access to a mobile phone network or local bank; and deliver cash directly through those accounts. The sooner we figure out how to deliver it safely, securely, and fast, the better.

Let Me Work

The idea that refugees can be contributors to the country in which they stay, not a burden, is fundamental to rethinking the humanitarian aid effort. To illustrate the point, here is the story not of a computer programmer or farmer or factory worker; it is the story of a beekeeper.

When refugees flee, they often say, they take their most prized possessions. For Um Laith and Abu Karam, from Dara'a in southwest Syria, that was impossible because their most prized possessions were bees. They had a very successful honey business inherited from their parents. Arriving in Jordan, with one son remaining in Syria to finish high school, Um Laith said she "felt like I was on a boat amid a storm."

Now they can see dry land, thanks to a $700 grant that has given them the chance to restart their business, albeit with Jordanian bees. Shyly, almost coyly, Mr. Karam asked if I would like to see his bees. He took me across the road from his apartment outside town to an olive grove sloping down and away from the apartment blocks. There were three beehives, small white huts that were the beginning of his new business.

He carefully approached the hives and took off the tops to reveal his precious swarms. They were his future—a source of finance as well as pride, a way of grounding himself in his new community.

If you understand that large numbers of refugees will not be going home, the obvious question is how—and where—they can earn a living and contribute to society. The best option is for adult refugees to be able to work—in the cities, towns, and rural areas of their host country. That way they can contribute to their own well-being and to the country in which they are living.

This is a huge political challenge. Just think of the rancor in Western countries when there are debates about immigrants taking jobs. That becomes acute when middle-income countries have unemployment problems of their own—which they often do.

Uganda has shown what is possible. By the end of 2016, nearly a million Congolese, South Sudanese, Burundian, and Somali refugees were living there. In 2017, South Sudanese were arriving at a rate of two thousand a day. They have the right to work, to move where they want, and to choose where to live. They are granted small plots of land to farm. They can access public services, send their children to public schools, build their skills, and make active contributions to the Ugandan economy by working, employing, and trading.

The country's economy is under tremendous strain from the surge of South Sudanese arrivals. But a 2014 study in Kampala found that 78 percent of refugees needed no aid, and nationwide only 1 percent were completely dependent on aid, because of the measures taken to help them work.[3] With the fifth-largest number of refugees in the world, Uganda's system clearly reveals the benefits of treating refugees as productive residents. The lessons will hopefully be spread more widely, because Uganda has been chosen to trial a new Comprehensive Refugee Response Framework, set up by the UN General Assembly in 2017 and designed to establish a new model of refugee support.

Critical to refugee employment is a bargain that offers extra support to countries hosting refugees. The economic hit from refugee influx on a large scale over a short period is real. Jordan, for example, has seen its debt-to-GDP ratio go from under 60 percent to above 90 percent. So the countries concerned need economic help.

The president of the World Bank, Jim Yong Kim, has recognized the importance of this issue and transformed the bank's attitude toward countries hosting refugees. (Previously middle-income countries were barred from receiving bank help.) In 2016, he pledged to develop new financial tools, including lower-cost financing and insurance products, to support the creation of jobs in countries hosting refugees. The aim in the Middle East is to generate 200,000 job opportunities for Syrian refugees in Jordan and more than a million in the region over the next five years.

There are parallels here from the past. For example, after the Second World War the US secretary of state, George

Marshall, announced the Marshall Plan to utilize public
finance and private enterprise to support the reconstruction
of Europe. It was supported by a range of security, political,
educational, and cultural commitments. And it was avowedly
launched as a four-year plan. The cost to the US taxpayer was
between 5 and 10 percent of the federal budget over the life of
the program. In cash terms it has been estimated at $120 billion
in current dollar value.

That kind of ambition is what is needed today—not from one
country but from the wider international community. Get this
right, and one other difficult question has a clear answer: the
future of humanitarian aid cannot be based on refugee camps.
They simply don't offer the chance for fulfilled lives. Instead of
places of refuge they become funeral homes for dreams.

Please, Please, Please Give My Kids a Chance: Give Them an Education

Nearly half of all displaced people are children. When I visited
Gaza in 2012 with Save the Children, it was the multitude of
vibrant, animated, ambitious youth that left its mark on me.
Around the world, visit any refugee camp, informal settlement,
or family in an urban setting, and children are everywhere.
Their parents talk of their hopes for their children, because
they have often lost hope for themselves.

Then there are the children without parents. I met seventeen-
year-old Frederick in the Nyarugusu refugee camp in Tanzania,

near the border with Burundi. The civil war in that country has claimed 300,000 lives.[4] On one side of the main road are the Congolese refugees, on the other the Burundians.

I remember Frederick because of his plaintive focus on the one thing that he thought could change his life: education. He sat in front of me in a tent on a bench with a dozen or so of his peers. He had a black school bag. He was well-spoken and very determined. He explained that it was the second time he had been expelled from Burundi to live in that "jail." He said he needed one more year of education in Burundi to get his high school diploma. He had one question: "Where can I get one more year of education, so that I can graduate with a recognized certificate?" I didn't have a good answer. His parting words stay with me: "I pray that I do not end my days here."

H. G. Wells said, "Human history becomes more and more a race between education and catastrophe." He was writing after the First World War. At the time, education and enlightenment were the alternative to disruption and disaster. His argument holds true today.

This is nowhere more true than among displaced people, where the absence of effective education is a catastrophe in the making. The figures speak for themselves. Around half of all displaced people are under the age of eighteen. And less than 2 percent of total humanitarian spending is on education.[5]

This is a recipe for disaster—not just impoverished lives but the risks of child labor, early marriage, even radicalization. And parents know it. As I was told by a Syrian refugee in Iraq in

March 2017, "I am going to go to Europe for my children. If I die on the way, I don't mind. At least they will get an education."

Brain imaging has shown how adversity such as displacement causes "toxic stress."[6] That makes stable, safe schooling that builds social and emotional skills vital in the midst of chaos—because there is also evidence that the damage can be reversed.

The best solution for children is clearly that they be enrolled in a local education system that is high quality and has the capacity to sustain itself despite the challenge of extra children with extra needs. Success comes with extra support—for example, language needs, tutoring, or additional psychosocial activities. Lebanon has created a "second-shift" system, under which schools conduct a second set of classes in the afternoon.

But what about where there is no education system? Or where the schools are full? Lebanon has done well to get 200,000 Syrian kids into school, but at least that number of others in the country are not getting any education at all. The European Union has pledged to raise education spending to 6 percent of its total humanitarian aid. That is a big increase compared to current levels but needs to become a much more thoroughgoing global movement to invest in the future.

Community-based education—sometimes called informal education—is the best bet for complementing state-based efforts in terms of impact and value for money. This is because it puts a premium on funding the human contact between teachers and children rather than focusing on new school buildings and other costly items. It is vital that nonformal education be considered a part of comprehensive national policy and that such schools be accredited and provide pathways to formal schooling. And in places where the mainstream system does not include certain children—girls, for example—nonformal education is a lifeline.

Protect Women and Children from Violence

The high politics of war and peace has an analog in the humanitarian sector, in the micropolitics of daily personal and intimate violence directed against women and girls. Peacemaking cannot just be something for (male) politicians, diplomats, and soldiers to do—not least because evidence shows that the involvement of women in peacemaking makes it more likely to succeed. While it is difficult to obtain a statistically significant sample, some studies suggest that increasing the proportion of women peacekeepers from 0 to 5 percent reduces the expected count of allegations regarding sexual exploitation and abuse by one half.[7] There is also a very practical and daily version of the high-level discussion of peacekeeping, peacemaking, and peace building in efforts to prevent and treat violence against women and girls. I want to highlight it here, because it is so much a feature of the humanitarian landscape, because the violence against women and girls so very much offends the foundations of decency and dignity, and because there is hardly a conversation with a refugee family where it is not hovering in the air.

In conflict situations, women and girls suffer the violent consequences of deeply unequal gender norms exacerbated by the breakup of families and communities, the weakening of community institutions, the prevalence of financial instability, and high levels of stress. Increased violence, including but not limited to sexual violence against women and girls, is closely linked to and heightened by displacement and manifests in a multitude of ways. Adolescent girls are particularly at risk of sexual violence, abuse, and exploitation and forced or early marriage.

Despite or maybe because of the extreme circumstances, basic interventions can make a big difference. For example, a study in the Dadaab refugee camp showed that rapes decreased by 45 percent during periods when houses were fully stocked with firewood (as opposed to women going to collect it and facing danger on the way).[8] Yet funding for dedicated interventions directed to the prevention and treatment of violence against women and girls, notably gender-based violence (GBV), is miserly. GBV programming receives only 0.5 percent of all humanitarian funding. This makes no sense, especially when it is clear that even with the worst trauma there is a capacity for recovery. DRC is known for high levels of violence, and one study showed that cognitive processing therapy sessions for survivors of sexual violence, delivered by women with no formal mental health training, greatly reduced depression, anxiety, PTSD, and functional impairment.[9]

When combined with economic interventions, there is a double dividend: an economic boost and a reduction in violence. When women's economic opportunity is improved, many studies have found better health in the family, increased schooling, and general improvement of women's protection. Economic programs paired with programs that address behavior change have also reduced intimate-partner violence.

I have also seen some successful attempts to *prevent* violence against women and girls—and that necessarily involves men. In Myebon, in Rakhine state, Myanmar, I saw life inside an enormous fenced area for one of the most victimized groups in the world today: the Muslim-minority population of Myanmar, the Rohingya. They make up around one-third of the population of Rakhine state but face displacement, violence, and rejection.

The settlement is so big that it incorporates preexisting villages. Electricity is intermittent to negligible, sanitary facilities brutally basic. But I also saw what it means to take violence against women seriously—by engaging Rohingya men.

In a prefabricated hut I met women learning about self-defense, and I also met husbands and sons committing themselves to leading the community in reducing violence against wives, daughters, and sisters. They are taught by (mainly) local aid workers and volunteers and role-play how to intervene in and prevent violence. Research shows that interventions like this—that are community based and multifaceted, involve both women and men, address the stigma associated with violence against women and girls, and focus on conflict resolution skills—can work. In countries such as Thailand, DRC, Haiti, and Kenya, such programs have successfully decreased the acceptance of violence against women and increased the acceptance of equal gender norms.

However, it remains the case that too often the most basic steps to reduce risks to women and girls are not taken. There are refugee camps without proper lighting, latrines without locks, food distribution that requires women to traverse unsafe ground. It makes you want to bang your head against the wall that this remains the case, but we need to turn that anger into action to reduce those risks.

For aid programs to be designed with a mind-set dedicated to reducing gender-based violence, we need the agencies in charge to be held to account. That means those that deliver food, cash, health care, or shelter should follow established good practice to minimize violence against women and girls; collect and publish data on the way in which basic risk-reduction measures are being taken; and ensure that women and girls are able to report violence and receive treatment for it. Appropriate data should be a tool used by donors to secure safer environments for women and girls.

Violence against women and girls reflects some of the deepest social and cultural inequalities of human history. No society is free of it. And the fact that too often it is the norm is no reason to look the other way. Words are not enough. There is no excuse for the mismatch of rhetoric and action that is all too evident. Hopefully this will be the century that makes greater strides toward real equality than any other—but we cannot afford to wait a century. Tackling violence against women and girls should be part of the wide, thoroughgoing economic and social change that women, and men, are advocating for around the world.

Better Aid in a Better System

The humanitarian enterprise involves moments of genuine heroism. And the gratitude from those who receive help is profound. But refugees and displaced people need more than heroism. They need an effective system of support—and at the moment it does not exist.

The most shocking thing about the aid system is not that it is too small—although that is a big issue. The biggest problems are the lack of agreed-upon goals; the weakness of the evidence base to drive programs; and the short-term nature of the grants that pay for interventions, which increases inefficiency and decreases innovation. All need to change.

At the moment, the individual efforts are extraordinary but the systems are weak. Different government donors decide their own priorities and their own procedures for distributing money. Different providers of health care, education, protection, or employment support have their own ways of doing things. Different UN agencies answer to different priorities and masters. And there are only weak benchmarks against which to plan provision and measure progress.

Yes, there are global sustainable development goals, set by the member states of the United Nations. They call for great accomplishments such as "inclusive and equitable quality education for all." The goals are universal and aspirational. And there are some important targets and indicators under each of the goals. But there are not specific targets for refugees and displaced people in different parts of the world—and there need to be, or the accountability and pressure for progress will not be strong enough.

What I would like to see is clear, quantifiable, and measurable targets for the outcomes from aid delivery for different affected populations—whoever the providers of help may be. Those targets would transcend the divide between humanitarian and development players in any location. They would apply to all. Funding and accountability would then be aligned behind those goals.

I saw the power of clear target setting when I was minister for schools. We had nationwide targets for improvement in exam scores. But we were concerned that averages could hide large inequalities, above all underperformance of the poorest children in the poorest communities. So we set "floor targets"—minimum levels of achievement—even in the most deprived schools.

The effect was significant. It was the use of floor targets, among other measures, that helped London move from being one of the poorest-performing school systems in the country to being one of the best. I think the idea of outcome targets for refugees and displaced people in different locations could achieve a similar impact.[10] It could focus different providers on shared goals; allow tracking of and intervention in areas of underperformance; and give refugees and displaced people some expectations against which to judge those who are helping them.

I accept that targets for improvement are worthless without the means to achieve them. The most important thing is to devise programs suited to needs and location.

I saw the power of hard data to save lives when I visited IRC programs for combating pneumonia in South Sudan in 2015. This disease kills nearly a million children worldwide every year. Crucial to reducing that number is effective and early diagnosis. For that reason community health workers had been given a pretimed one-minute alarm clock and directed to count the number of breaths of children who had a cough or difficulty breathing. More than fifty breaths per minute in an infant or forty in an older child meant that pneumonia was present.

But the rate of effective assessment was only 26 percent. The reason? Many of the workers could not count or remember the two cutoff numbers. The answer is not to sack the workers. These are communities with very small numbers of numerate people. There is a better way.

The IRC created and distributed "counting beads," necklaces with color-coded beads. The beads were red above fifty (forty for older children) and thereby signified a pneumonia case. By showing the workers how to move one bead per breath, the need for counting and remembering was removed. The rate of proper assessment—placing their finger within plus or minus three beads of where the clinician had counted—was raised to 66 percent. Today, 4,500 community health workers supported by the IRC in South Sudan and Democratic Republic of Congo are using counting beads.

This kind of commitment to testing and using what works needs to be used across the humanitarian sector. Yet when it comes to reducing child mortality, preventing family violence, promoting refugee employment, and extending education, the humanitarian community lacks enough hard evidence about what works best. Laurence Chandy and his colleagues concluded that when it comes to the overlap between displacement and poverty, "cutting-edge knowledge is blunt and . . . best-practice solutions feel decidedly under-whelming."[11] To date there have been around 100 impact evaluations of policies and practices in conflict settings, compared with more than 4,500 in poor but stable countries. This isn't healthy, because although crisis situations can make research harder, it is precisely their life-and-death challenges that make it important to get real data on what works.

Crucially, funding needs to follow the evidence: programs with high levels of impact need to receive more funds. This kind of commitment can make aid money go further, which, in a world of constrained resources, means saving and changing more lives.

A study in Kenya showed that a single investment of $8,900 could improve the reading skills of 100 students by 20 percent if the money were spent on computer-assisted literacy instruction. But the same amount of money could get the same result for 423 students if it were spent on performance incentives for teachers and for 695 students if it were spent on remedial tutoring.[12] That's six times as many students who could be helped than via technology alone. Not every study will expose that kind of variation, but the process of comparing the cost-effectiveness of different approaches should be widespread.

If you buy the argument that we need clearer outcomes and more evidence of what works, the question is how to make them the norm. Just as in government or the private sector, it is money that drives behavior. Reform of the financial system is vital to achieving greater impact. The current flow of money is unpredictable, the speed of delivery way too slow. And we are trying to tackle multigenerational problems with short-term grants.

I know that at the IRC, our international programs in 2016 were worth about $570 million. They were spread across around 400 grants—and at the end of the year another 160 grant proposals were in the pipeline. So you can see the fragmentation, as well as the short-termism: the average grant length was for around twelve months.

We need multiyear grants to match the duration of the problems. But that is not the end of it. Pooling of funds across agencies (humanitarian, development) and across sectors (health care, education for women and children) would make sure that money follows needs. In addition, we need to look at whether insurance products can be adapted to unlock new capital and speed up responses to the most severe crises. That is in the hands of the donors and can be done—if there is the will.

There is one other example of the new kind of financing we need: capital for programs that could achieve transformative impact but equally might fail. In the private sector this would be called research and development (R&D). In that sector investment is 5 percent of turnover. That would mean $1.3 billion for the humanitarian sector. But only a fraction of that amount is going into R&D at the moment.[13] The reason is partly lack of funds overall, which means that urgent needs drive out important longer-term research. There is also a natural wariness about taking risks with some of the world's most vulnerable people. But I am talking about taking risks *for* beneficiaries.

We know there are severe problems that need new thinking and that a string of potential solutions could be drawn from other sectors. Now is the time for risk capital to go into large and thoughtful investments with potentially transformative impact.

Put into practice, these ideas would free up time and money in humanitarian work and above all increase its impact. They are about disciplined policy making, priority setting, and budget making. They have a practical core idea: to turn humanitarian action into a system that will change the lives of displaced people in the most powerful way possible—indeed, change our global future.

I have never seen a contradiction between being hardheaded and being big-hearted. The two must go together.

4 Refugees Welcome

Refugees and the countries that host them desperately need our financial support. But we cannot just give them money and turn away. We also need to welcome refugees to our own shores. Help needs to start here, on the home front. We need to expand fair and humane ways of offering sanctuary to people who are fleeing for their lives.

Starting a new life in a new country is hard. But we know from evidence and experience that refugees, who have survived horrendous strife, know deeply the meaning of freedom and are determined to offer their children the life chances they were denied or had removed.

One of the first people to benefit from the IRC's refugee services after the Soviet invasion of Hungary in 1956 was a young refugee named András Gróf. We diagnosed that he needed a hearing aid, because of scarlet fever he had suffered as a child—and bought him one. He went from strength to strength, eventually founding Intel and thereby transforming all of our lives. Few refugees have the impact of Andy Grove, the name he later took, but by virtue of their experience refugees have something special to offer.

So "Refugees Welcome" is not just a slogan; it is a statement of principle and purpose. It is precisely because not everyone can be offered refuge that the rules need to be fair. I know this from my own family history.

After the Second World War, my grandfather went back to Belgium to find his wife and daughter, with the aim of returning with them to the United Kingdom to join my dad, who had returned to student life. The decision lay in the hands of Home Secretary James Chuter Ede. It looked as though we would be lucky. There was powerful support for the application, because my dad's tutor at the London School of Economics was Harold Laski, then chairman of the governing Labour Party.

The letters from Harold Laski begin "My Dear Chuter" and make the case for the Milibands to be allowed to come and join their outstanding young relative in Britain. Today this would be called "family reunification" and remains important. Yet as seemingly well positioned as my relatives were, the answer was negative. Ede's replies were friendly but firm: not everyone who wants to come can do so, he said, and there can be no favoritism. He actually used the now-toxic word *flooded*.

You can see Ede's dilemma: he had a tough enough job sorting out who could come, so he could not start allocating places to please a colleague. (There is one irony to the story: by an extraordinary twist of fate, Ede was member of Parliament for South Shields, the constituency I would come to represent fifty years later.)

When refugees are given protection in a new country, it gives them a chance to restart their lives. But that's not the only reason to admit refugees. Welcoming refugees is a symbolic stand with the countries that host the most refugees. And by accepting refugees we uphold individual rights in international law, a foundation of the global order that needs to be defended.

Today there are a range of routes by which refugees find safety. I focus here on the two most significant routes to the West for refugees: resettlement and asylum.

Refugee resettlement occurs when a government agrees that a refugee can be transferred to its country to give him or her sanctuary. The vetting of the person for a "well-founded fear of persecution," for assessment of his or her vulnerability, for security checks, takes place outside the country. The United States has traditionally had the largest refugee resettlement program.

Asylum, by contrast, occurs when a government agrees that someone can *stay* in its country. The test, including security vetting to determine whether someone should be allowed to stay because he or she cannot safely be returned home, occurs in the country or at the border. Germany now has the largest asylum program in the world.[1]

Both refugee resettlement and asylum are important. Resettlement needs to be expanded; asylum systems need to be better and more humanely organized.

Refugee Resettlement: A Long Road to Freedom

Bushra Naji is typical of the refugees who are being resettled. She and her family are from Baghdad. She was an elementary school teacher, and her husband was an engineer. Her eldest son, Zaid, was targeted and shot by Shia militia in 2004 (he was twenty-two at the time), and her second son, Omar, was kidnapped multiple times. She and her family fled to the Yarmouk refugee camp outside Damascus, Syria, and lived there in a single room for two years. From there they applied for refugee resettlement in the United States. They were admitted in 2008.

They found the cost of living in the Bronx, New York, prohibitively high, so they moved to Idaho for two years, and the parents worked in a potato factory. The family then moved back to New York, where Bushra got a job working for the IRC. Her husband, Tarik, works for a power-supply company. Their children are all working, from HR to computing to a Jewish charity. Meanwhile, her nephew is in the US military.

The last time we spoke, Bushra said she is proud to be an American. She is completely committed to the country. Her children say that they never forget the privilege they have been given. You could not want a better neighbor.

Resettlement gives refugees the chance to start a new life in a stable country and is nothing short of a lifesaver for those in need. It targets the most vulnerable refugees, including women at risk, disabled or ill children, elderly refugees, and victims of torture. The gateway to the process is most often policed by UNHCR, but receiving nations run their own security and other vetting processes and retain full rights to pick and choose whom they will take. Individuals who have committed serious crimes, obviously including terrorist acts, are excluded from refugee status and are therefore not eligible for resettlement.

In 2016, fewer than 200,000 people were formally resettled through the refugee resettlement process around the world.[2] The four main countries of origin were Syria (one-third of the total), DRC, Iraq, and Somalia. The United States has traditionally taken the largest number (around 40 to 50 percent of the total), but the Trump administration has pledged to reduce the number to a maximum of 50,000. In the calendar year 2016, Canada was the next highest, with nearly 47,000, followed by Australia (27,600) and the United Kingdom (5,000).

Refugee resettlement programs have proved wrong the doomsters who say refugees cannot be successfully integrated. In the United States, the IRC and other resettlement agencies meet refugees at the airport and help them find housing and work, get the kids into school, and start their new life. The US system puts a premium on refugees getting jobs straightaway. The government loans refugees money to pay travel costs and gives them cash support for a few months to pay for housing, food, and personal necessities. After a year they can get a green card, and after five years they can become citizens. A recent study estimates that refugees pay $21,000 more in taxes than they receive in benefits over their first twenty years in the United States.[3]

There are other models of refugee resettlement that galvanize citizen action. In Canada, "private sponsorship" allows families or groups of people to promise to support, from their own pocket, refugees for a year (to the tune of $28,000 Canadian for a family of four). Recent research shows that refugees in Canada do attain a middle-class lifestyle, although they often take a decade to get there.[4] A similar "community sponsorship" scheme is being piloted in the United Kingdom with the support of voluntary organizations and faith-based groups

In 2016, thirty-seven countries participated in refugee resettlement. Given the UN estimate that nearly 1.2 million vulnerable refugees have special and urgent need for resettlement, the number of countries resettling refugees, as well as the number they resettle, has to increase—the opposite of the Trump administration's proposal to cut the number of refugees admitted.

European countries collectively resettled just over 14,000 refugees in 2016—up from 9,000 the year before but still very low. The IRC calculates that Europe should increase its number significantly by taking a minimum of 540,000 refugees over five years through a legal resettlement program.

The proposal for a European Union–wide resettlement scheme is now making its way through the European Parliament and Council of Ministers. Done right, this long-overdue reform could greatly improve the coordination of national efforts, speed up the process of resettlement, and increase the numbers of those resettled.

In addition, none of the Gulf Cooperation Council countries is currently accepting refugees. Although they have many Syrians living and working in their countries, they do not host them or resettle them as refugees. They should sign the UN convention and start to do so.

Security Vetting for Refugee Resettlement

Though it is completely legitimate for people to say they want proper security screening of refugees, it is not legitimate for those who have the facts at their disposal to distort them in an effort to demonize refugees as a security threat. In fact, refugees undergoing resettlement face tougher security checks than do people applying for student or tourist visas. It is wrong to make victims of terror pay twice over for the actions of terrorists, first when they lose everything in war or conflict, then by denying them a chance to restart their lives.

There are at least twenty-one steps in the US vetting process for screening Syrian refugees. The process takes an average of eighteen to twenty-four months for all refugees and involves twelve to fifteen government agencies conducting multiple checks, biometric tests, and in-person interviews to ensure that refugees are who they say they are and pose no threat to the United States.

When countries fall victim to the temptation to keep refugees out, they offer a propaganda gift to those who would foment extremism. That is what the successive executive orders on immigration and refugees, signed by President Trump in January and March 2017, have done.

The executive orders defined danger by nationality; confused immigration visas, whose vetting is lighter, with refugee visas, whose vetting is already very tough; sold short Iraqis who had supported the US military and government; and thereby gave an easy win to those who would whisper to Muslims around the world that the United States would never have their back. Whether or not the executive orders are finally deemed contrary to the Constitution, they are certainly contrary to common sense and good policy making. No wonder Daesh-friendly channels on social media described the ban as "blessed."[5]

A series of independent reports has tried to make sense of the publicly available data on refugees and terrorism. A former FBI analyst, Nora Ellingsen, says there have been four FBI arrests of refugees on terrorism-related offenses, including two from the list of countries on President Trump's executive order (neither was planning terrorism in the United States). The New America Foundation says that "every jihadist who conducted a lethal attack inside the United States since 9/11 was a citizen or legal resident." The Heritage Foundation explains that incomplete data make it impossible to make an exact determination, but when it included refugees from before 2002, it counted sixty-one who had engaged in Islamist terrorist activities.[6]

More than 900,000 refugees have been admitted for resettlement into the United States since 9/11. The Cato Institute calculated in September 2016 that Americans had a one-in-3.64-billion chance of being killed by a refugee.[7] So-called homegrown terrorism is a far greater danger, and that is not the preserve of any one group or religion.

At every stage there is no right for refugees to be resettled; they are dependent on the choices of the resettlement countries. As the most recently retired US secretary of homeland security, Jeh Johnson, said, "It is always the applicant's burden of proof to demonstrate that he or she qualifies for refugee status in this country. . . . If we do not have information to reach a sound decision, or the application raises questions not satisfactorily addressed, the case is put on hold until we have more, or is denied."[8]

The US administration is well within its rights to review the vetting arrangements for refugees. It does not need to suspend the refugee admissions program to do so. If there is scope for sensible administrative changes, they should be made. That has been going on year after year in any case. But once the administration has satisfied itself about the vetting, what is the logic of the president's decision to cut the annual number of refugees admitted into the United States from 110,000 under the plans left by President Barack Obama to 50,000? There is none.

Asylum claimants, in contrast to those going through refugee resettlement, do not wait in Jordan, Kenya, or Congo, or in Syria as Bushra Naji did, for their application to be processed. They make their own way to a country that is a signatory to the UN Refugee Convention and then claim asylum, either at the border or in the country. As civil conflicts proliferate, climate change kicks in, and the gap between humanitarian need and provision grows, more people are likely to flee and claim asylum.

The trauma faced by unaccompanied minors from the Central American triangle of Honduras, Guatemala, and El Salvador is the American version of this tragedy. On the way to Europe, more than 13,000 people have died in the Mediterranean since the start of 2015.[9] Of the ones who survive, many have been stripped of their savings by smugglers. Still others have been separated from their families and abused on the route, and some have been imprisoned in terrible conditions. I remember in Lesvos, Greece, meeting an elderly Syrian woman whose wheelchair had been thrown into the Aegean Sea by people smugglers as surplus to requirements and not covered by her fee. Fortunately, the IRC was able to buy her a new wheelchair, but others are not so lucky.

And there is no guarantee that their claim will be successful: the numbers vary among countries, but overall around 40 percent of the total number of asylum claims are rejected.[10]

During 2016, 2.2 million people in 164 countries submitted asylum claims, 200,000 fewer than the previous year. There were 262,000 in the United States, mainly from Central America. Continuing the trend established in 2015, Germany received the most claims: 722,000 in total.[11] In total, 2.5 million asylum claims were submitted in Europe in 2015 and 2016.[12]

British prime minister Theresa May has tried to argue that generosity to asylum seekers is not fair to those who cannot make the journey, but who are we to say that an asylum seeker from Aleppo, applying in the United Kingdom, has less need than a refugee seeking resettlement from Jordan? The right to seek asylum has been hard-won and represents a commitment to upholding individual rights and due process in international law. Refugees and host countries need a fast, efficient, consistent system for processing claims, integrating those who qualify, and safely and humanely returning home those who do not.

Asylum: It Is Right and Needs to Be Better Organized

Europe's experience shows in stark form the challenges of managing asylum. Its geographic proximity to conflict and poverty hot spots in the Middle East and North Africa makes it a natural magnet. The distribution of responsibilities between

European and national institutions, and the relationship between free movement within the European Union and restrictions at its borders, adds a complicating factor. Europe is committed to high standards of human rights but does not have the level of integration or cooperation among member states that makes for smooth or effective management.

The European Union says boldly that "migration is both an opportunity and a challenge."[13] That makes sense. Some states have a real need to boost their labor force with foreign-born workers. Meanwhile, however, undocumented and underdocumented economic migrants and asylum seekers have arrived in large numbers and are concentrated in a few member states. So there is a significant challenge, too.

Germany's response has been bold, brave, and, I would argue, successful. It is easy to criticize Chancellor Angela Merkel and her coalition colleagues for lack of planning before she announced that Germany would allow all Syrian asylum seekers to stay and have their asylum claims processed (rather than return them to their first country of arrival into the European Union). The risks of ignoring the refugee crisis on Europe's doorstep outweighed those of the action she took. And the power of an effective state, with tremendous volunteer effort across the country, has made extraordinary strides to get on top of the issue.

In February 2016, I went to Berlin to meet Chancellor Merkel and some refugee families. The night before, Mrs. Merkel's plane had developed engine trouble while she was returning from election campaigning, so she had not had much sleep, but she presented a calm and committed approach to her mantra "*Wir schaffen das*" (more or less "We can do this"). She explained that as someone who had grown up in East Germany, she had a strong sense of the conflicting feelings of loss and hope that the refugees were feeling. She emphasized that Germany was a rich country with a unique history that spurred amazing voluntary action among residents to come out and help. She was so proud of her fellow citizens: they clearly inspired her, despite the opposition her actions had generated and the fears of an electoral backlash. She conveyed an inner calm that if Germany could reunite East and West, incorporating tens of millions of citizens into a single country, it could deal with a million asylum claims.

As of the spring of 2017, the numbers arriving in the European Union from the Middle East were significantly down—from around 2,000 a day in the first quarter of 2016 to around 350 a day in the first quarter of 2017.[14] There are a variety of reasons for this fall, including the impact of a deal struck between the European Union and Turkey, under which Turkey imposed tighter border restrictions on refugees attempting to reach Europe and agreed to take back all refugees arriving on the Greek islands. However, the pressure on the route from North Africa, primarily Libya, to Italy and Spain is very high. Sixty thousand people arrived in Italy in the first five months of the year and joined the queues in centers waiting for processing.

The scale of the challenge, both political and practical, is evidenced by the fact that the following are even being discussed: whether it is wrong to rescue people from the sea, because of the danger that it will encourage others to come; whether it is acceptable to return people to Libya, where there is no government and they face grave danger; whether to use development money for security to tackle migration flows rather than to tackle poverty.

My answer to each of these questions is no. But however much European leadership on humanitarian aid improves conditions for refugees in Africa and the Middle East, Europe faces fundamental choices about how to honor its commitment to an effective asylum system in a way that is enforceable, manageable, and acceptable.

There are a range of issues at the external border of Europe. The European Union has recently agreed upon a new entry-exit system that will record the movements (and refusals of entry) of all third-country nationals into and out of the European Union. This is essential as a security measure. But that is only one side of the story. What goes on inside the borders needs to be addressed, too.

At the end of 2016, there were 140,000 outstanding applications for asylum in Greece and Italy, the two countries that receive the large bulk of Europe's asylum seekers.[15] Those people are waiting in camps and processing centers to have their claims adjudicated. They must be properly processed with resolve and urgency. Europe's fundamental challenge is to develop a more integrated, better harmonized system of procedures, qualification conditions, and reception standards across the EU nations.

The Common European Asylum System makes the point. It requires applicants for protection to seek asylum in the country of first entry. That makes sense but is possible only if Italy and Greece are given processing support and guaranteed that they will not be expected to cater for all successful asylum claimants. That is the significance of the demand that all countries share responsibility, either by participating in a scheme for distributing successful asylum seekers across the continent or by paying others to look after those they refuse to take.

Those who do not qualify for asylum, because they are not judged to face a well-founded fear of persecution if they are returned home, need to be safely and humanely returned to their country of origin, as a vital measure for the integrity and acceptability of the asylum process. The latest European figures are from 2015, when around 250,000 failed asylum seekers, not all those slated for return, but a serious commitment, were sent back to their country of origin. Those people should not be treated like criminals—because they aren't.

The European experience has global lessons. Where the protections for those on the move are weakly enforced, they need to be strengthened. Where they are ignored, they need to be asserted. Where processing is slow and haphazard, it needs to be speeded up and made consistent. Where conditions are inhumane, they need to be improved. When applications fail, people need to be returned home with dignity. And where refugees and asylum seekers are welcomed, they need to be integrated. Arrival is only the start; integration is the goal. It takes both to make for success in a diverse society.

Protection and Integration

Those of us who defend the rights of refugees and asylum seekers need to be the first, not the last, to insist on effective screening, appropriate orientation, and thorough integration. Pope Francis, who defends refugees and asylum seekers at every opportunity, has written, "I think that, in theory, hearts must not be closed to refugees, but those who govern need prudence. They must be very open to receiving refugees, but they also have to calculate how best to settle them, because refugees must not only be accepted, but also integrated."[16]

The word *integration* needs to be used advisedly and deliberately. It should be demanding as well as empowering but will do its job only if it is understood for what it is, as well as what it is not. For me, it is critically linked to the idea of inclusion and unity. Integration means joining in a common endeavor. It involves contribution to shared tasks. It suggests mutual responsibility and commonweal.

Integration to me has a different meaning from *assimilation*. To Americans I think there may be a different meaning, but *assimilation*, to European ears, suggests that the new arrival is absorbed into a preexisting, static culture in which he or she sheds all previous identity. That is neither desirable nor possible. Integration is different, too, however, from the ideal of tolerance, which connotes to me the separation of a new arrival from the community he or she is joining. In fact, *tolerance* carries little connotation of joining anything.

A recent study by the McKinsey Global Institute highlights the four keys to successful integration. They put labor market measures to get people into jobs first; emphasize the importance of education for children; highlight the significance of housing that is integrated, not ghettoized; and underscore the importance of learning the local language and culture.[17]

That mirrors the IRC experience in the United States. Economic integration—from jobs to building a credit history—is the foundation. But alone it is not enough. Social integration, from schooling to housing to community life, is key to success.

One of the United Kingdom's most successful home secretaries, Roy Jenkins, addressed this point in his first speech on the job fifty years ago. He was prescient about the challenges. Strongly defending the expansion of Commonwealth immigration into the United Kingdom, he argued that it was folly to try to "turn everybody out in a common mould . . . a series of carbon copies of someone's misplaced version of the stereotyped Englishman." He also warned against an "embittered sense of apartness." He called for integration "not as a flattening process of assimilation, but as equal opportunity, accompanied by cultural diversity."[18]

The lesson that Jenkins took from the United States was that integration requires positive action. That is more true today than ever.

Where there is grievance, it needs to be addressed by engagement. Where there is crisis of identity, it is best met by showing that there does not need to be a choice between religion and nationality. Where there is charismatic recruitment to extremist groups, it needs more than effective counterterrorism measures; it needs community mobilization to isolate and diminish the attraction.

In the end, integration is up to all of us. It takes effort, street by street. That is how barriers are broken down and communities are built. It is the story of progress throughout the ages. It is needed now more than ever.

5 Conclusion

Ubuntu . . . we belong in a bundle of life. We say, "A person is a person through other persons."

—Archbishop Desmond Tutu

The biggest obstacle we face in the refugee crisis is not the scale of the problem but the sapping, nagging fear that we can't make a dent. It is easy to feel that the issue is too large, too complex, too far gone to make a difference. Whenever that thought creeps in, I look at a crayon drawing in my office in New York. It was given to me when I was in northeast Nigeria by an eleven-year-old girl named Amina Musa.

The violence there, in a region of historic immense poverty, is driven by Boko Haram, which terrorizes the local population. I visited Malakhoi settlement outside Yola, the capital of Adamawa state. In a clearing of some trees and grassland—trampled to dust—were some mud huts. Trees marked a place where children were benefiting from the IRC's "healing classroom," an approach that uses play, instruction, and classroom management to create safe, structured places for learning that help children come to terms with the emotional and social consequences of conflict. There were blue and green blankets on the floor, some tables and chairs, and a lot of children.

That is where I met Amina Musa. She was small and seated on a white plastic chair, crowded around a small white plastic table with half a dozen other children. She was completely focused on the picture she was drawing of a Nigerian woman. The outline of the face and upper body was done in pencil. There were earrings, a headdress, and a choker necklace with a heart-shaped pendant. Then there were pastel colors drawn in crayon: turquoise, orange, yellow, green.

Amina explained that it was her image of beauty. She couldn't tell me if it was a woman she knew or just someone she had dreamt of. But her teachers told me that only eleven weeks before, all she could draw were dead bodies and soldiers. They wanted me to take the picture as an example of what is possible. If Amina Musa can make that kind of recovery, we owe it to her and millions like her to give them a chance of rebuilding their lives.

We Are Crew

The displacement crisis is not just a policy problem for governments. It is a test for all of us, both in business and as private citizens. There is an imperative to step up. As the futurist Marshall McLuhan once said, "There are no passengers on Spaceship Earth. We are all crew."[1] And when governments fail to see the danger of a course they are on, it often requires the voluntary sector, faith-based communities, and the private sector and private citizens to take a lead.

Fortunately, there are many ways for people to make their humanity count. We must start with the refugees who arrive in our communities. They need your local knowledge—of everything from how the bus system works to where to find a doctor. They need your language skills—to practice and become proficient. They need your networks—to help find a job. They need support for their kids—befriending your children and adjusting to a new life. They need in-kind help— clothing, furniture, home goods—because they arrive with debts, not money.

There is nothing like an invitation to your home. Recently, my family had a refugee family from Bhutan over for dinner. They arrived in New York City two years ago after twenty-five years in a refugee camp in Nepal. We asked what they thought when they landed. They said, "No words." They were dignified and courageous and we felt proud to have them in our home. Airbnb's "Open Homes program"—a program that encourages the company's hosts to open their homes for free to refugees—is one way to participate. You can read about it at www.airbnb.com/welcome/refugees. If you live in Europe, you can also organize your own dinner at www.unitedinvitations.org.

Refugees will warm to an invitation from your church, synagogue, temple, or mosque. In January 2017, I took Nargis, a Muslim refugee from Afghanistan resettled by the IRC, to a service at New York's Central Synagogue. There must have been five hundred people in attendance. In the middle of the service she told her story of abuse at the hands of her husband, flight from Afghanistan, and eventual resettlement in the United States. Suddenly there was a connection. From connection came understanding. And from understanding, voluntary action to support refugees.

You can read about opportunities to help refugees in the United States at www.welcomingamerica.org /engage/take-action. In the United Kingdom, go to www.refugee-action.org.uk/heres-can-help-refugees, www.refugees-welcome.org.uk, or www.cityofsanctuary.org. In Sweden, visit www.welcomemovement.se or www.oppnadorren.se. In Germany, you can volunteer at your local branch of the Save Me Kampagne: Type "save me" and your town or neighborhood. In the Netherlands, visit www.vluchtelingenwerk.nl/steun-ons.

Refugees also need your voice—on social media and with your elected representatives—to stand up for international aid for fragile states hosting refugees as well as for refugee resettlement. For too long the assumption of cross-party support has led to neglect of the need to explain and persuade. It takes courage to stand up, but it is so much easier when you get support. The example of US mayors of cities in states that have tried to ban refugees—places such as Dallas, Houston, and Midland in Texas—shows that support of refugees does not need to mean political death. You can join the coalition in the United States at Welcoming America, www.welcomingamerica.org.

Business is vital to this drive. Of course refugees start businesses and employ people. But for other businesses, there is one overriding requirement. It is about core business, not charity: Help refugees into work. There are many examples of this. The commitment of Starbucks to hire 10,000 refugees is the most noteworthy and sets a benchmark. But in truth every business in every sector has the potential to make a contribution.

This is partly about mind-set. Lawyers turned up at airports to help refugees caught by the Trump administration's travel ban in January 2017. In higher education, Zach Messitte, the president of Ripon College, a small liberal arts college in Wisconsin, called me a few years ago, ready to offer scholarships to refugees thanks to support from an alumnus. He was keen to work with the IRC to find students. This year the first student, Mherete Mherete from Ethiopia, graduated through the program, majoring in economics and business. He played on the soccer team, joined a fraternity, and is now deciding among three job offers in Chicago and Washington, DC. The message Messitte sent me was simple: "Please send us more students like Mherete!"

There are many good examples of how business can step up—not just with money but by granting leave to employees with ideas and experience. Google has provided technical support for an information platform for refugees arriving in Europe (www.refugee.info). Another good example is Starwood Hotels & Resorts Worldwide, working with TripAdvisor. In 2016, Starwood helped the IRC develop and launch Hospitality Link, a robust job-readiness program to provide refugees resettled in Dallas, Texas, and San Diego, California, with quality employment in the hospitality sector. The program has now expanded to three other cities with the support of TripAdvisor Charitable Foundation.

The message for businesses large and small is: Give what you can, mobilize your staff to do the same, hire refugees, and think about how to apply your skills, technology, or systems to the refugee issue. For more inspiration, look here: www.tentpartnership.org.

Commentators often talk about the backlash against refugees. And, yes, there certainly is fearmongering and abuse. But backlash is only half the story. There is also support—as people step up to defend the values on which their countries have been built. That is what the ice cream company Ben & Jerry's is doing with its campaign for refugee resettlement in Europe. For every person who is afraid of a refugee, there is someone who wants to offer a welcome. There is a discussion to be had, and now is the time to have it.

Both individuals and businesses need to step up as governments consider stepping back. I wouldn't be doing my job if I didn't say that NGOs depend on private and business support. Since I am British, it doesn't come naturally to talk about fund-raising, but four years in New York have given me practice. You can donate to the IRC at www.rescue.org. I would love it if you did. We will put the money into improving services for refugees and displaced people around the world.

Our Shared Future

The refugee and displacement crisis is not just another policy problem that needs to be solved. It is a moral and political fork in the road: moral because each of us has to decide what we think and what we are going to do; political because the treatment of refugees goes to the heart of the purpose and nature of the global order and the role of the countries in it; fork in the road because the assumptions and institutions that have been fundamental to global progress in the last seventy years are now under challenge in the very countries that helped create that order in the first place.

The treatment of refugees is a weather vane of the character, stability, and values of the international system. We *can* rescue the dignity and hopes of refugees and displaced people, and if we do so we will help them and in the process restore our own values and international purpose. The goal is to mitigate the suffering of those displaced and release their human potential. But the benefit should be a material difference to the stability of the international order and a practical demonstration of the benefits of international cooperation.

When countries are confident, strong, and self-aware, as Western countries were after the Second World War, they are open to and engaged with the world. They help the most vulnerable beyond their shores out of humanity and a sense of responsibility but also out of self-interest.

The West after World War II stood for what John F. Kennedy called a "declaration of interdependence"; asserted universal values, not just Western ones; and argued that injustice or oppression anywhere was a threat to justice and freedom everywhere. Rights for refugees were of a piece with the drive of the Cold War to break down walls.

That commitment is now at stake. Globalization is too unequal, too unstable, and too insecure for its own good. The displacement crisis is part of that syndrome. And the crisis is being exploited by those who would tear down the global system, not reform it.

When countries are fearful or doubtful, lacking vision and direction, they close up, even to people whose stories would make your heart melt. That is happening in the West today. The US administration proposes a double whammy: Reduce overseas aid and cut the number of refugees allowed to come. European countries are struggling to agree on a coherent policy framework. Britain has decided to revoke invitations to 3,000 unaccompanied refugee children to settle in the United Kingdom.

The opposition to help for refugees is symptomatic of a wider crisis of confidence, from trade to security to climate. President Trump's withdrawal from the Paris Climate Accord, and particularly his explanation of the decision, set out an alternative view of the world to the "declaration of interdependence." In his speech announcing the decision to withdraw, there is no notion of a world community facing shared problems. There are only competing nations with singular interests; if one wins, another must lose. The notion of a "public good," where the benefits of an action cannot be restricted to the country that takes it but that are essential to all, is lost.

This position is often called "populist," because it pits the interests of "ordinary people" against the elite. As Jan-Werner Müller, a professor of politics at Princeton University, explained in his important book on populism,[2] the populism of the right takes central aim at foreigners as a threat to "the people," sidestepping any economic assault on the privileges of the elite. He identifies three sides to the populist equation on the right: "the people," who are being betrayed by "the elite," which is favoring foreigners for its own reasons.

In this brand of politics, the real anger at economic and social loss among working and middle-class people, and at the gaping and growing inequalities between the richest and the rest, is channeled into animus toward some of the most vulnerable people in the world. President Trump explicitly uses this tactic. He said in a statement to mark his hundredth day in office, "Year after year, you pleaded for Washington to enforce our laws as illegal immigration surged, refugees flooded in, and lax vetting threatened your family's safety and security."

In this statement you have the dehumanization of refugees—the "flood." There is the weaponization of refugees—by saying that they are potential poison. And any legitimate claim to sanctuary is undermined by blurring the lines between refugees and immigrants.

The danger should be clear: that new walls define the first half of the twenty-first century in the way the Iron Curtain defined the second half of the twentieth. They reflect an international system in disrepair: weaker multilateral institutions, more erratic unilateral démarches by countries with the ability to enforce their will, more disorder in the global commons. Thus the inequalities and insecurities that fueled the backlash against the multilateral system are exacerbated rather than addressed.

My view is simple: globalization without rules is not viable; without institutions is not manageable; without fairness is not legitimate. So we need to double down on renewing the flawed but essential international system.

This alternative to the vicious circle of vilification and retreat requires not just new political messaging—different threats, different villains, different heroes—but also a new way of thinking. That goes well beyond refugees and displaced people. It needs to recognize where the global order has become a victim of its own success, such as in expanding markets or spurring technological innovation, both of which have spurred a backlash, and where it has been a victim of its own failures in curbing inequality, in Iraq and Afghanistan, in addressing the climate crisis. It needs to square the circle between satisfying a sense of identity and belonging without offering the "alternative fact" (actually unrealizable fact) of a return to a better yesterday.

This is a fight for international cooperation over unilateral grandstanding, for the benefits of pluralism over the tyranny of groupthink, and for the enduring importance of universal values over the slicing and dicing of populations and religions in a fake and faulty clash of civilizations. It is a fight for values, insights, and institutions that imperfectly uphold the best of human nature in the face of impulses and arguments that humor the worst.

The fate of refugees and displaced people depends on this effort. That is why it is a bellwether for the future of the international order. It is a test case for whether the idea of an international community, joined by common humanity, is real or meaningless. Look after the most vulnerable, by upholding their rights, and you don't just help them, you set a benchmark for the way shared problems are tackled. You establish mutual responsibility as a founding principle of international relations. And you set the stage for tackling other problems, from climate change to health risks.

The inequalities and insecurities of this period of globalization are embodied by the trials of displaced people. Their needs are acute, their sense of rejection deep. The scale and scope of the crisis are precisely why they are a good test—of our values and of our vision. It's not just a test we need to pass; it is a test we can pass together, if we all play a part.

Syrian refugee children learn in an informal tented settlement in Lebanon.

ACKNOWLEDGMENTS

I am indebted to the late Ed Victor, literary advocate, not just agent, who helped me get onto paper my aspirations for this book and who found my editor, Michelle Quint at TED Books. She has been unfailingly enthusiastic and consistently right, even when dispensing tough love (her first edit called for an "overhaul"). I am also grateful to two friends in London, Peter Hyman and Charlie Leadbeater, who helped me conceive and plan the project.

I have been very fortunate in my colleagues at the IRC. Their generosity in offering encouragement and expertise has made the book possible. I am delighted that every sale will deliver finance to support our work. The cochairs of the IRC's board of directors, Katherine Farley and Tracy Wolstencraft, said I should pursue the project. Denise Felloni somehow managed to carve out, and protect, time for me to work on the book. Kate Cornelius helped her keep my office running. I am immensely grateful to Sarah Case, who has been a tremendous research, planning, and thought partner, contributing ideas and insights all the way through the process. Daniele Ressler joined the team to help me cover areas where I knew too little and find and check facts where I had only an intuition of what was true. The following colleagues also read and commented on the book: Jeannie Annan, Yolanda Barbera, Kristen Kim Bart, Ricardo Castro, Ciaran Donnelly, Alyoscia d'Onofrio, Grant Gordon, Anna Greene, Ravi Gurumurthy, Oliver Money, Jodi Nelson, Radha Rajkotia, Madlin Sadler, Elinor Raikes, Jennifer

Sime, Sarah Smith, Imogen Sudbery, Rachel Unkovic, and Melanie Ward. Karl Pike kindly read through a late draft and made helpful suggestions.

I have dedicated this book to my family. Louise makes everything worthwhile, and the boys give everything perspective. The greatest thanks are due to the three of them.

INTRODUCTION

1   Where only first names are used, I have changed them at the request of the family to protect their identity.

2   UNHCR, *Global Trends: Forced Displacement in 2015* (Geneva: UNHCR, 2016); http://www.unhcr.org/576408cd7.pdf.

3   Ibid.

4   Richard Haass has published a book by this title: *A World in Disarray: American Foreign Policy and the Crisis of the Old Order* (New York: Penguin, 2017).

5   David Armitage, *Civil Wars: A History in Ideas* (New York: Knopf, 2017).

6   Bremmer, "The Era of American Global Leadership Is Over. Here's What Comes Next," *Time*, December 19, 2016; http://time.com/4606071/american-global -leadership-is-over/.

CHAPTER 1: THE CRISIS

1   UNHCR, *Global Trends: Forced Displacement in 2016*. (Geneva: UNHCR, 2016); http://www.unhcr.org/5943e8a34.pdf.

2   World Bank Group, *Forcibly Displaced: Toward a Development Approach Supporting Refugees, the Internally Displaced, and Their Hosts* (Washington, DC: World Bank Group, 2017); https://openknowledge.worldbank.org/bitstream /handle/10986/25016/9781464809385.pdf?sequence=11&isAllowed=y. See also Nicholas Crawford, John Cosgrave, Simone Haysom, and Nadine Walicki, *Protracted Displacement: Uncertain Paths to Self-reliance in Exile* (London: Overseas Development Institute, September 2015); https://www.odi.org/sites/odi .org.uk/files/odi-assets/publications-opinion-files/9851.pdf.

3   Xavier Devictor and Quy-Toan Do, "How Many Years Have Refugees Been in Exile?," Policy Research Working Paper WPS7810 (Washington, DC: World Bank Group, 2016); http://documents.worldbank.org/curated/en/549261472764700982 /How-many-years-have-refugees-been-in-exile.

4   David Armitage, *Civil Wars: A History in Ideas* (New York: Knopf, 2017).

5   Ibid.

6   UNHCR, *Global Trends: Forced Displacement in 2016*, 15; http://www.unhcr
    .org/5943e8a34.pdf.

7   "Syria Regional Refugee Response—Lebanon"; http://data.unhcr.org/syrianrefugees
    /country.php?id=122. See also UNRWA Lebanon page, https://www.unrwa.org/sites
    /default/files/content/resources/unrwa_in_figures_2016.pdf.

8   UNHCR, *Global Trends: Forced Displacement in 2016*: http://www.unhcr
    .org/5943e8a34.pdf.

9   Norwegian Refugee Council, *Grid 2017: Global Report on Internal Displacement*
    (Geneva: Internal Displacement Monitoring Centre, 2017), 9; http://www.internal
    -displacement.org/assets/publications/2017/20170522-GRID.pdf.

10 World Bank, "World Bank Forecasts Global Poverty to Fall Below 10% for First
    Time; Major Hurdles Remain in Goal to End Poverty by 2030," October 4, 2015;
    http://www.worldbank.org/en/news/press-release/2015/10/04/world-bank
    -forecasts-global-poverty-to-fall-below-10-for-first-time-major-hurdles-remain-in
    -goal-to-end-poverty-by-2030.

11 Our World in Data, "Share of the World Population Living in Absolute Poverty,
    1820–2015"; https://ourworldindata.org/wp-content/uploads/2013/05/World
    -Poverty-Since-1820.png.

12 "GDP (current US $)"; http://data.worldbank.org/indicator/NY.GDP.MKTP.CD.

13 Laurence Chandy, Hiroshi Kato, and Homi Kharas, "From a Billion to Zero: Three
    Key Ingredients to End Extreme Poverty," in *The Last Mile in Ending Extreme
    Poverty*, ed. Chandy et al. (Washington, DC: Brookings Institution Press, 2015),
    6–17.

14 Ibid., 14.

15 Simon Maxwell, "A New Case Must Be Made for Aid. It Rests on Three Legs,"
    March 28, 2017; https://oxfamblogs.org/fp2p/a-new-case-must-be-made
    -for-aid-it-rests-on-three-legs/.

16 Paolo Verme, Chiara Gigliarano, Christina Wieser, Kerren Hedlund, Marc Petzoldt,
    and Marco Santacroce, *The Welfare of Syrian Refugees: Evidence from Lebanon and
    Jordan* (Washington, DC: World Bank, 2016), xi; https://openknowledge
    .worldbank.org/bitstream/handle/10986/23228/ 9781464807701
    .pdf?sequence=21.

17 Elizabeth Ferris, "Climate Change, Migration, and the Incredibly Complicated Task of Influencing Policy," Keynote Address, Brookings Institution Conference on "Human Migration and the Environment: Futures, Politics, Invention," Durham University, Durham, UK, July 2015; http://cmsny.org/publications/climate-change -migration-policy-ferris/.

18 Norwegian Refugee Council, *Grid 2017: Global Report on Internal Displacement*, (Geneva: Internal Displacement Monitoring Centre, 2017), 10; http://www .internal-displacement.org/assets/publications/2017/20170522-GRID.pdf.

19 Ban Ki Moon, "A Climate Culprit in Darfur," *Washington Post,* June 16, 2007; http://www.washingtonpost.com/wp-dyn/content/article/2007/06/15 /AR2007061501857.html.

20 Caitlin E. Werrell, Francesco Femia, and Troy Sternberg, "Did We See It Coming? State Fragility, Climate Vulnerability, and the Uprisings in Syria and Egypt," *SAIS Review of International Affairs* 35, no. 1 (Winter–Spring 2015): 32; http://research .fit.edu/sealevelriselibrary/documents/doc_mgr/463/Werrell%20et%20al.%20 %202015.%20%20CC%20Middle%20East.pdf. See also Colin P. Kelley, Shahrzad Mohtadi, Mark A. Cane, Richard Seager, and Yochanan Kushnir, "Climate Change in the Fertile Crescent and Implications of the Recent Syrian Drought," *PNAS* 112, no. 11 (March 17, 2015): 3241–46; http://www.pnas.org/content/112/11/3241.full.

21 R. Andreas Kraemer et al., "Building Global Governance for 'Climate Refugees,'" March 18, 2017; http://www.g20-insights.org/demo/policy_briefs/building-global -governance-climate-refugees/.

22 Colin Bundy, "Migrants, Refugees, History and Precedents," *Forced Migration Review* 51 (January 2016); http://www.fmreview.org/sites/fmr/files /FMRdownloads/en/destination-europe/bundy.pdf.

23 UNHCR, "Convention and Protocol Relating to the Status of Refugees" (Geneva: UNHCR, 2010); http://www.unhcr.org/en-us/3b66c2aa10.

24 Gilbert Jaeger, "On the History of the International Protection of Refugees," *International Review of the Red Cross* 83, no. 843 (September 2001): 727–38; https://www.icrc.org/eng/assets/files/other/727_738_jaeger.pdf.

25 UNHCR, "States Parties to the 1951 Convention Relating to the Status of Refugees and the 1967 Protocol"; http://www.unhcr.org/en-us/protection /basic/3b73b0d63/states-parties-1951-convention-its-1967-protocol.html.

26 International Organization for Migration, "Global Migration Trends 2015 Factsheet"; http://publications.iom.int/system/files/global_migration _trends_2015_factsheet.pdf.

27 Susan Nicolai et al., "Education Cannot Wait: Proposing a Fund for Education in Emergencies" (London: Overseas Development Institute, May 2016), 10; https:// www.odi.org/sites/odi.org.uk/files/resource-documents/10497.pdf. See also UNHCR, "Missing Out: Refugee Education in Crisis," September 2016; http:// www.unhcr.org/57d9d01d0.

28 Paolo Verme et al., *The Welfare of Syrian Refugees: Evidence from Lebanon and Jordan*, 8; https://openknowledge.worldbank.org/bitstream /handle/10986/23228/ 9781464807701.pdf?sequence=21.

29 Department for International Development, "CHASE Briefing Paper: Violence Against Women and Girls in Humanitarian Emergencies," October 2013, 8; http://reliefweb.int/sites/reliefweb.int/files/resources/VAWG-humanitarian -emergencies.pdf.

30 High-Level Panel on Humanitarian Financing, "Report to the Secretary-General: Too Important to Fail—Addressing the Humanitarian Financing Gap," January 2016, 2; http://reliefweb.int/sites/reliefweb.int/files/resources/%5BHLP%20 Report%5D%20Too%20important%20to%20fail%E2%80%94addressing%20 the%20humanitarian%20financing%20gap.pdf.

31 "Syria Conflict: Jordanians 'at Boiling Point' over Refugees," BBC, February 2, 2016; http://www.bbc.com/news/world-middle-east-35462698.

32 United Nations, "Universal Declaration of Human Rights"; http://www.un.org/en /universal-declaration-human-rights/.

33 Albert Einstein to Eleanor Roosevelt, July 26, 1941. Franklin D. Roosevelt Presidential Library and Museum; https://fdrlibrary.tumblr.com /post/141047307759/i-have-noted-with-great-satisfaction-that-you.

34 Ishaan Tharoor, "What Americans Thought of Jewish Refugees on the Eve of World War II," *Washington Post*, November 17, 2015; https://www.washingtonpost.com /news/worldviews/wp/2015/11/17/what-americans-thought-of-jewish-refugees -on-the-eve-of-world-war-ii/?utm_term=.480596f89b87.

CHAPTER 2: WHY WE SHOULD CARE

1 Ryan Teague Beckwith, "Transcript: Read the Speech Pope Francis Gave to Congress," *Time*, September 24, 2015; http://time.com/4048176 /pope-francis-us-visit-congress-transcript/.

2 Jim Yardley, "Pope Francis Takes 12 Refugees Back to Vatican After Trip to Greece," *New York Times*, April 16, 2016; https://www.nytimes.com/2016/04/17/world /europe/pope-francis-visits-lesbos-heart-of-europes-refugee-crisis.html?_r=0.

3 "Archbishop of Canterbury on the Refugee Crisis," September 3, 2015; http://www.archbishopofcanterbury.org/articles.php/5606 /archbishop-of-canterbury-on-the-migrant-crisis.

4 Ed Stetzer, "Evangelicals, We Cannot Let Alternative Facts Drive U.S. Refugee Policy," *Washington Post*, January 26, 2017; https://www.washingtonpost.com /news/acts-of-faith/wp/2017/01/26/evangelicals-we-cannot-let-alternative-facts -drive-u-s-refugee-policy/?utm_term=.b12175ca64c1&wpisrc=nl_faith&wpmm=1.

5 Jonathan Sacks, *Not In God's Name: Confronting Religious Violence* (New York: Schocken Books, 2015), 186–87.

6 Omid Safi, "Faith and History Demand Better of Us," On Being, January 26, 2017; https://onbeing.org/blog/omid-safi-faith-and-history-demand-better/.

7 "Refugee Act of 1979: Hearings Before the Subcommittee on Immigration, Refugees, and International Law of the Committee on the Judiciary, House of Representatives, Ninety-Sixth Congress, First Session, on H.R. 2816," 222. U.S. Government Printing Office, Washington, DC: 1979; https://archive.org/stream /refugeeactof1979000unit#page/220/mode/2up/search/califano.

8 Joschka Fischer, "Goodbye to the West," Project Syndicate, December 5, 2016; https://www.project-syndicate.org/commentary/goodbye-to-american-global -leadership-by-joschka-fischer-2016-12.

9 Ian Buruma, "The End of the Anglo-American Order," *New York Times*, November 29, 2016; https://www.nytimes.com/2016/11/29/magazine/the-end-of-the-anglo -american-order.html.

10 Tal Kopan, "Donald Trump: Syrian Refugees a 'Trojan Horse,'" CNN Politics, November 16, 2015; http://www.cnn.com/2015/11/16/politics /donald-trump-syrian-refugees/.

11 Adam Nossiter, "Marine Le Pen, French National Front Leader, Speaks at Her Hate-Speech Trial," *New York Times*, October 20, 2015. https://www.nytimes .com/2015/10/21/world/europe/marine-le-pen-french-national-front-leader -speaks-at-her-hate-speech-trial.html.

12 "Wilders Tells Dutch Parliament Refugee Crisis Is 'Islamic Invasion,'" *Newsweek*, September 10, 2015; http://europe.newsweek.com/wilders-tells-dutch-parliament -refugee-crisis-islamic-invasion-332778. See also Sarah Wildman, "Geert Wilders, the Islamophobe Some Call the Dutch Donald Trump, Explained," Vox, March 15, 2017; http://www.vox.com/world/2017/3/14/14921614/geert-wilders -islamophobia-islam-netherlands-populism-europe.

13 From George Washington to Joshua Holmes, December 2, 1783, https://founders .archives.gov/documents/Washington/99-01-02-12127.

14 See, e.g., "How to End the War in Afghanistan," *New York Review of Books*, April 29, 2010; http://www.nybooks.com/articles/2010/04/29/how-to-end-the-war -in-afghanistan/.

15 UNHCR, *Global Trends: Forced Displacement in 2016* (Geneva: UNHCR, 2017); http://www.unhcr.org/5943e8a34.pdf.

16 Christopher de Bellaigue, *The Islamic Enlightenment: The Struggle Between Faith and Reason, 1798 to Modern Times* (New York: Liveright Publishing, 2017), 351.

17 Peter Neumann, *Radicalized: New Jihadists and the Threat to the West* (London: I. B. Tauris, 2016).

18 Thomas Gibbons-Neff, "'Fear of Muslims Is Rational': What Trump's New National Security Adviser Has Said Online," *Washington Post*, November 18, 2016.; https:// www.washingtonpost.com/news/checkpoint/wp/2016/11/18/trumps-new -national-security-adviser-has-said-some-incendiary-things-on-the -internet/?utm_term=.e1329d245a76.

19 Ahmed Rashid, "ISIS: What the US Doesn't Understand," *New York Review of Books*, December 2, 2014. http://www.nybooks.com/daily/2014/12/02 /isis-what-us-doesnt-understand/.

20 Ed Husain, "Wrecking Ramadan: What Happened to the Month of Peace?," CNN, June 24, 2017: http://www.cnn.com/2017/06/24/opinions/isis-ramadan-month -of-peace/index.html.

21 See, e.g., Marwan Muasher, *The Second Arab Awakening and the Battle for Pluralism* (New Haven, CT: Yale University Press, 2014).

22 Michael V. Hayden, "Former CIA Chief: Trump's Travel Ban Hurts American Spies—and America," *Fresno Bee*, February 6, 2017: http://www.fresnobee.com /opinion/opn-columns-blogs/article131060334.html?fb_comment_id=1464539040 283588_1464548310282661.

CHAPTER 3: THE RENEWAL OF RESCUE

1   Department for International Development, "Annual Report and Accounts 2015–16"; https://www.gov.uk/government/uploads/system/uploads/attachment_data /file/538878/annual-report-accounts-201516a.pdf.

2   International Rescue Committee, "Emergency Economies: The Impact of Cash Assistance in Lebanon," August 1, 2014; https://www.rescue.org/report /emergency-economies-impact-cash-assistance-lebanon.

3   Alexander Betts, Louise Bloom, Josiah Kaplan, and Naohiko Omata, "Refugee Economies: Rethinking Popular Assumptions" (Oxford, UK: Humanitarian Innovation Project, University of Oxford, June 2014), 36–37; https://www.rsc.ox.ac .uk/files/publications/other/refugee-economies-2014.pdf.

4   Murithi Mutiga, "Burundi Civil War Fears as President Accused of Campaign of Murder," *Guardian*, January 5, 2016; https://www.theguardian.com/world/2016 /jan/05/burundi-pierre-nkurunziza-police-protest-crack-down.

5   Susan Nicolai et al., "Education Cannot Wait: Proposing a Fund for Education in Emergencies" (London: Overseas Development Institute, May 2016), 8; https:// www.odi.org/sites/odi.org.uk/files/resource-documents/10497.pdf.

6   J. P. Shonkoff et al., "The Lifelong Effects of Early Childhood Adversity and Toxic Stress," *Pediatrics* 129(1): e232–e246.

7   Charles Kenny, "Using Financial Incentives to Increase the Number of Women in UN Peacekeeping," October 17, 2016: https://www.cgdev.org/publication /using-financial-incentives-increase-number-women-un-peacekeeping.

8   Maureen Murphy, Diana Arango, Amber Hill, Manuel Contreras, Mairi MacRae, and Mary Ellsberg, "Evidence Brief: What Works to Prevent and Respond to Violence Against Women and Girls in Conflict and Humanitarian Settings?" (Washington, DC: George Washington University, 2016); http:// whatworks.co.za/documents/publications/66-maureen-murphy-diana -arango-amber-hill-manuel-contreras-mairi-macrae-mary-ellsberg/file.

9   Judith K. Bass et al., "Controlled Trial of Psychotherapy for Congolese Survivors of Sexual Violence," *New England Journal of Medicine*, 2013; 368 (June 6, 2013), 2182–91: DOI: 10.1056/NEJMoa1211853. http://www.nejm.org/doi/full/10.1056 /NEJMoa1211853#t=article.

10 The UN calls these "collective outcomes."

11 Laurence Chandy, Hiroshi Kato, and Homi Kharas, "From a Billion to Zero: Three Key Ingredients to End Extreme Poverty," in *The Last Mile in Ending Extreme Poverty*, ed. Chandy et al. (Washington, DC: Brookings Institution Press, 2015), 5.

12 Patrick J. McEwan, "Improving Learning in Primary Schools of Developing Countries," *Review of Educational Research* 85, no. 3 (September 1, 2015): 353–94.

13 Deloitte, "The Humanitarian R&D Imperative: How Other Sectors Overcame Impediments to Innovation," March 2015; https://www2.deloitte.com/content /dam/Deloitte/global/Documents/About-Deloitte/dttl_cr_humanitarian_r&d _imperative.pdf.

CHAPTER 4: REFUGEES WELCOME

1 UNHCR, *Global Trends: Forced Displacement in 2016* (Geneva: UNHCR, 2017); http://www.unhcr.org/5943e8a34.pdf.

2 Ibid.

3 William N. Evans and Daniel Fitzgerald, "The Economic and Social Outcomes of Refugees in the United States: Evidence from the ACS." National Bureau of Economic Research Working Paper No. 23498: http://www.nber.org/papers /w23498.

4 Lori Wilkinson and Joseph Garcea, "The Economic Integration of Refugees in Canada: A Mixed Record?," Migration Policy Institute, April 2017: http://www.migrationpolicy.org/research/economic-integration -refugees-canada-mixed-record.

5 Eliza Mackintosh, "Trump Ban Is Boon for Isis Recruitment, Former Jihadists and Experts Say," CNN Politics, January 31, 2017; http://www.cnn.com/2017/01/30 /politics/trump-ban-boosts-isis-recruitment/index.html.

6 Nora Ellingsen, "It's Not Foreigners Who Are Plotting Here: What the Data Really Show," Lawfare, February 7, 2017; https://lawfareblog.com/its-not-foreigners -who-are-plotting-here-what-data-really-show. "Part II. Who Are the Terrorists?," New America; https://www.newamerica.org/in-depth/terrorism-in-america/who -are-terrorists/. "The U.S. Refugee Admissions Program: A Roadmap for Reform," Heritage Foundation, July 5, 2017; http://www.heritage.org/immigration/report /the-us-refugee-admissions-program-roadmap-reform.

7 Alex Nowrasteh, "Terrorism and Immigration: A Risk Analysis," Cato Institute, September 13, 2016; https://www.cato.org/publications/policy-analysis /terrorism-immigration-risk-analysis.

8 Statement by Secretary Jeh C. Johnson on the Safety and Security of the Homeland, and How Congress Can Help, November 23, 2015; https://www.dhs .gov/news/2015/11/23/statement-secretary-jeh-c-johnson-safety-and-security -homeland-and-how-congress-can.

9 International Organization of Migration; https://missingmigrants.iom.int/. Accessed on August 14, 2017.

10 UNHCR, *Global Trends: Forced Displacement in 2016* (Geneva: UNHCR, 2017); 44–45; http://www.unhcr.org/5943e8a34.pdf.

11 Ibid.

12 Pew Research Center, March 15, 2016; http://www.pewresearch.org/fact-tank / 2017/03/15/european-asylum-applications-remained-near-record-levels-in-2016/.

13 European Union Delegation to the United Nations, "EU Statement—United Nations General Assembly: Special Session on Population and Development beyond 2014," September 22, 2014; http://eu-un.europa.eu/eu-statement-united-nations-general -assembly-special-session-on-population-and-development-beyond-2014/.

14 UNHCR, "Operational Data Portal"; http://data2.unhcr.org/en/situations /mediterranean.pdf.

15 UNHCR, *Global Trends: Forced Displacement in 2016* (Geneva: UNHCR, 2017); http://www.unhcr.org/5943e8a34.pdf.

16 Conferenza Stampa di Papa Francesco nel volo di ritorno dal Viaggio Apostolico in Svezia in occasione della Commemorazione Comune luterano-cattolica della Riforma, January 11, 2016 (English translation provided.); http://press.vatican.va /content/salastampa/it/bollettino/pubblico/2016/11/01/0789/01764.html#en.

17 McKinsey Global Institute, "Europe's New Refugees: A Road Map for Better Integration Outcomes," December 1, 2016; http://www.regionalmms.org/images /sector/a_road_map_for_integrating_refugees.pdf.

18 Roy Jenkins, *Essays & Speeches* (London: Collins, 1967).

CHAPTER 5: CONCLUSION

1 Statement in 1965, in reference to *Operating Manual for Spaceship Earth* (1963) by Buckminster Fuller, as quoted in *Paradigms Lost: Learning from Environmental Mistakes, Mishaps and Misdeeds* (2005) by Daniel A. Vallero, p. 367.

2 Jan-Werner Müller, *What Is Populism?* (Philadelphia: University of Pennsylvania Press, 2016).

ABOUT THE AUTHOR

David Miliband is president and CEO of the International Rescue Committee (IRC), where he oversees the agency's humanitarian relief operations in more than forty war-affected countries and its refugee resettlement and assistance programs in twenty-six United States cities.

From 2007 to 2010, Miliband was the 74th Secretary of State for Foreign Affairs of the United Kingdom, driving advancements in human rights and representing the UK throughout the world.

As the son of refugees, Miliband brings a personal commitment to the IRC's work. He lives in New York City with his wife, violinist Louise Shackelton, and their two sons.

David Miliband's TED Talk, available for free at TED.com, is the companion to *Rescue: Refugees and the Political Crisis of Our Time.*

PHOTO: BRET HARTMAN / TED

His Holiness Pope Francis
Why the only future worth building
includes everyone
A single individual is enough for
hope to exist, and that individual
can be you, says His Holiness Pope
Francis in this searing TED Talk
delivered directly from Vatican City.
In a hopeful message to people of
all faiths, to those who have power
as well as those who don't, the
spiritual leader provides illuminating
commentary on the world as we
currently find it and calls for equality,
solidarity, and tenderness to prevail.
"Let us help each other, all together,
to remember that the 'other' is not a
statistic, or a number," he says. "We
all need each other."

Melissa Fleming
A boat carrying 500 refugees sank at
sea. The story of two survivors
Aboard an overloaded ship carrying
more than 500 refugees, a young
woman becomes an unlikely hero.
This single, powerful story, told by
Melissa Fleming of the UN's refugee
agency, gives a human face to the
sheer numbers of human beings
trying to escape to better lives as the
refugee ships keep coming.

António Guterres
Refugees have the right to be
protected
António Guterres thinks that we can
solve the global refugee crisis—and
he offers compelling, surprising
reasons why we must try. In conversation with TED's Bruno Giussani,
Guterres discusses the historical
causes of the current crisis and
outlines the mood of the European
countries that are trying to screen,
shelter, and resettle hundreds of
thousands of desperate families.
Bigger picture: Guterres calls for a
multilateral turn toward acceptance
and respect—to defy the anti-refugee
propaganda and recruiting machines
of groups like ISIS.

Aala El-Khani
What it's like to be a parent in a war
zone
How do parents protect their children
and help them feel secure again
when their homes are ripped apart
by war? In this warmhearted talk,
psychologist Aala El-Khani shares
her work supporting—and learning
from—refugee families affected by
the civil war in Syria. She asks: How
can we help these loving parents give
their kids the warm, secure parenting
they most need?

The Great Questions of Tomorrow
by David Rothkopf

We are on the cusp of a sweeping revolution—one that will change every facet of our lives. The changes ahead will challenge and alter fundamental concepts such as national identity, human rights, money, and markets. In this pivotal, complicated moment, what are the great questions we need to ask to navigate our way forward?

Payoff
The Hidden Logic That Shapes Our Motivations
by Dan Ariely

Payoff investigates the true nature of motivation, our partial blindness to the way it works, and how we can bridge this gap. With studies that range from Intel to a kindergarten classroom, Dan Ariely digs deep to find the root of motivation—how it works and how we can use this knowledge to approach important choices in our own lives.

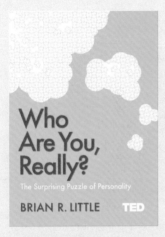

Who Are You, Really?
The Surprising Puzzle of Personality
by Brian Little

Who are you? Are you an introvert or extrovert? Agreeable or irritable? Chances are you probably have a pretty fixed idea of what makes you, you. But what if your personality was flexible, and ultimately in your control? Acclaimed psychologist Brian Little reveals that personality is far more malleable than we imagine.

The Terrorist's Son
A Story of Choice
by Zak Ebrahim

The astonishing first-person account of an American boy raised on dogma and hate—a boy presumed to follow in his father's footsteps—and the man who chose a different path. The idea that reverberates through the prose: Everyone has a choice. Even if you're raised to hate, you can choose tolerance. You can choose empathy.

TED is a nonprofit devoted to spreading ideas, usually in the form of short, powerful talks (eighteen minutes or less) but also through books, animation, radio programs, and events. TED began in 1984 as a conference where Technology, Entertainment, and Design converged, and today covers almost every topic—from science to business to global issues—in more than 100 languages. Meanwhile, independently run TEDx events help share ideas in communities around the world.

TED is a global community, welcoming people from every discipline and culture who seek a deeper understanding of the world. We believe passionately in the power of ideas to change attitudes, lives, and, ultimately, our future. On TED.com, we're building a clearinghouse of free knowledge from the world's most inspired thinkers—and a community of curious souls to engage with ideas and each other, both online and at TED and TEDx events around the world, all year long.

In fact, everything we do—from the TED Radio Hour to the projects sparked by the TED Prize, from the global TEDx community to the TED-Ed lesson series—is driven by this goal: How can we best spread great ideas?

TED is owned by a nonprofit, nonpartisan foundation.